FOO FIGHTERS

EASY GUITAR WITH NOTES & TAB

Cover photo © Andy Sheppard/Redferns

ISBN 978-1-4803-9736-1

HAL•LEONARD®

Visit Hal Leonard Online at
www.halleonard.com

Contact us:
Hal Leonard
7777 West Bluemound Road
Milwaukee, WI 53213
Email: info@halleonard.com

In Europe, contact:
Hal Leonard Europe Limited
42 Wigmore Street
Marylebone, London, W1U 2RN
Email: info@halleonardeurope.com

In Australia, contact:
Hal Leonard Australia Pty. Ltd.
4 Lentara Court
Cheltenham, Victoria, 3192 Australia
Email: info@halleonard.com.au

STRUM AND PICK PATTERNS

This chart contains the suggested strum and pick patterns that are referred to by number at the beginning of each song in this book. The symbols ⊓ and ∨ in the strum patterns refer to down and up strokes, respectively. The letters in the pick patterns indicate which right-hand fingers play which strings.

p = thumb
i = index finger
m = middle finger
a = ring finger

For example; Pick Pattern 2
is played: thumb - index - middle - ring

Strum Patterns

Pick Patterns

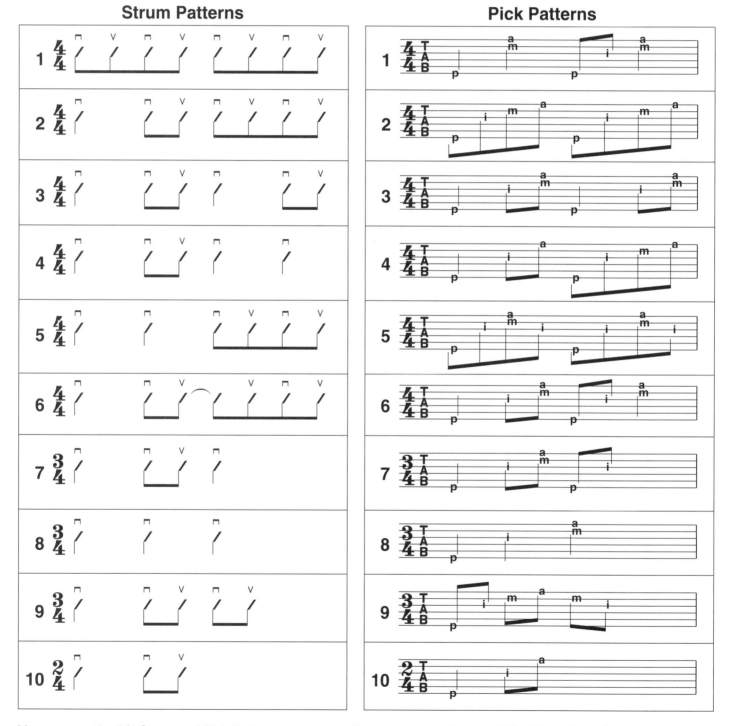

You can use the 3/4 Strum and Pick Patterns in songs written in compound meter (6/8, 9/8, 12/8, etc.).
For example, you can accompany a song in 6/8 by playing the 3/4 pattern twice in each measure.
The 4/4 Strum and Pick Patterns can be used for songs written in cut time (¢) by doubling the note
time values in the patterns. Each pattern would therefore last two measures in cut time.

All My Life

Words and Music by David Grohl, Christopher Shiflett, Oliver Taylor Hawkins and Nate Mendel

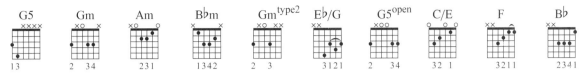

Strum Pattern: 6
Pick Pattern: 4

Intro
Moderately fast Rock

All my life I've been search-ing for some - thing. Some -

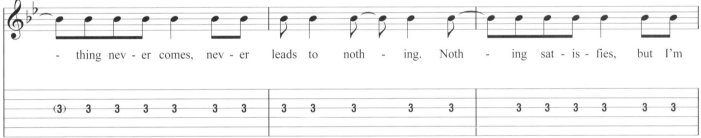

- thing nev - er comes, nev - er leads to noth - ing. Noth - ing sat - is - fies, but I'm

get - ting close, _ clos - er to the prize _ at the end of the rope. _

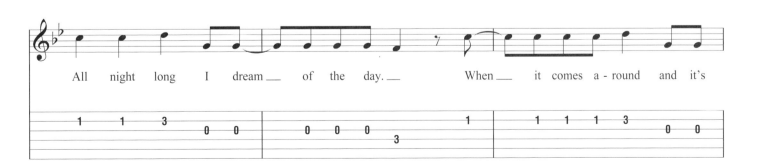

All night long I dream _ of the day. _ When _ it comes a - round and it's

tak - en a - way. ___ Leaves ___ me with the feel - ing that I feel the most, ___ feel ___

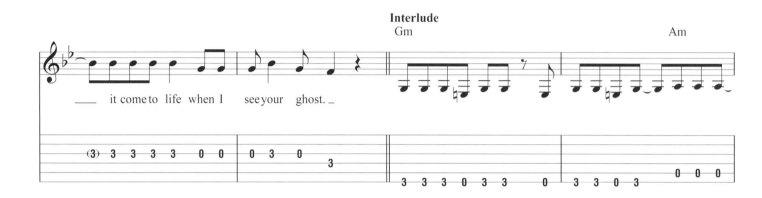

Interlude

___ it come to life when I see your ghost. ___

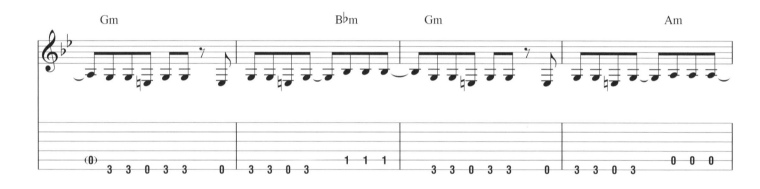

Verse

1. Calm down, ___ don't you re - sist.
2. *See additional lyrics*

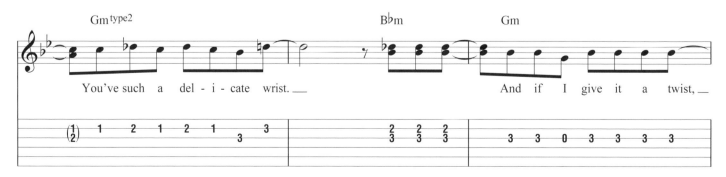

You've such a del - i - cate wrist. ___ And if I give it a twist,

4

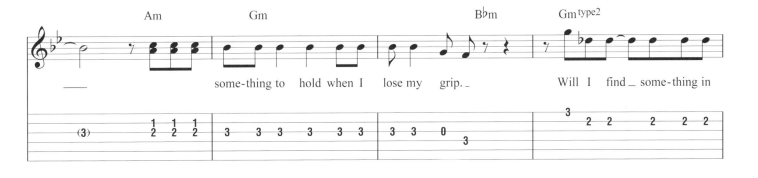

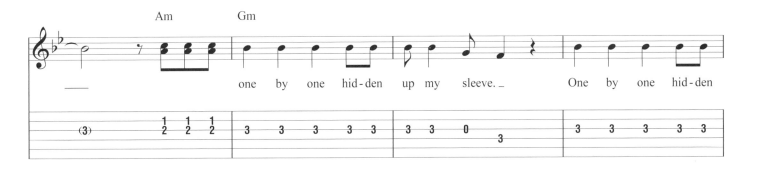

𝄋 Chorus

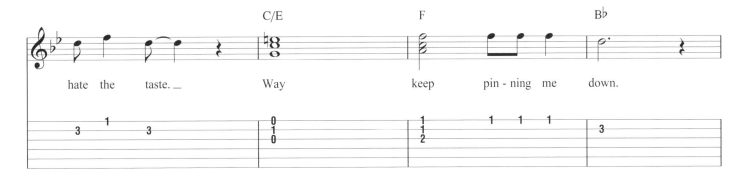

Eh, _____ don't let it go to waste, _ I love it, but I hate the taste. _

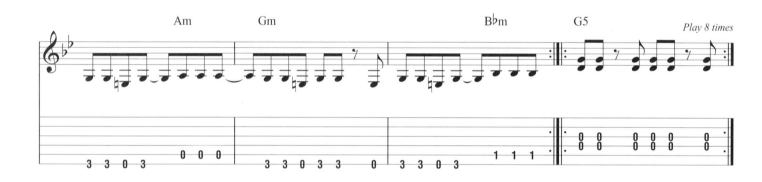

Way keep pin - ning me down. _____

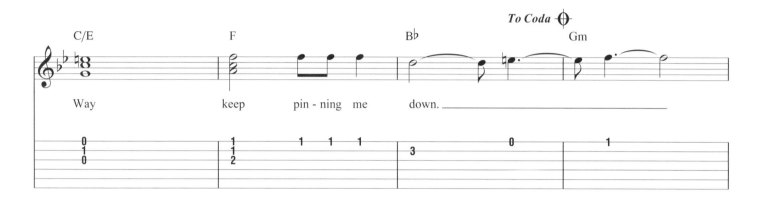

Play 8 times

Bridge

All my life I've been search-ing for some - thing. Some - thing nev - er comes, nev - er

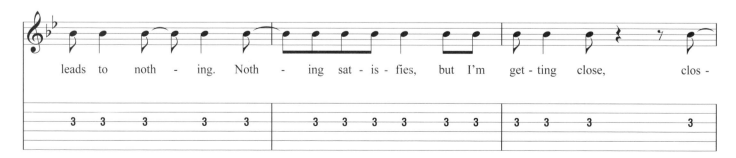

leads to noth - ing. Noth - ing sat - is - fies, but I'm get - ting close, clos -

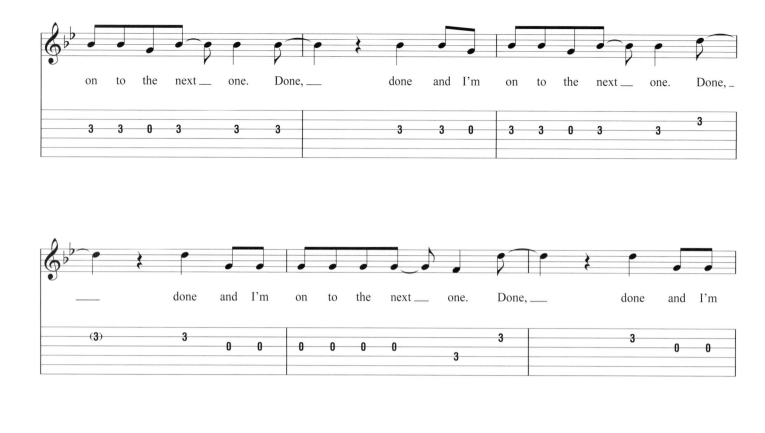

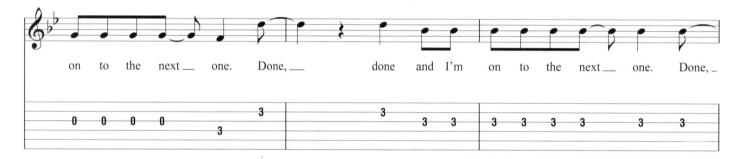

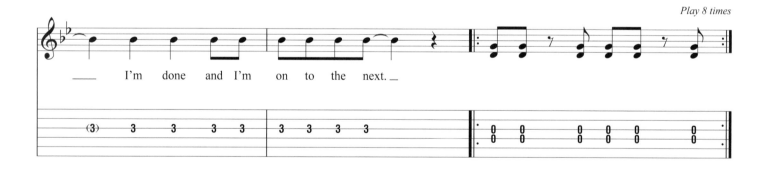

on to the next ___ one. Done, ___ done,   on to the next ___ one. Done, ___

D.S. al Coda   **Coda**

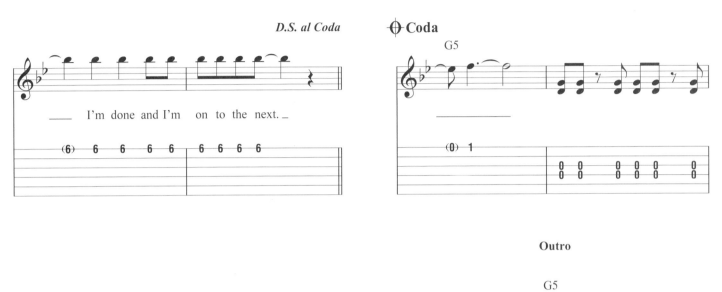

___ I'm done and I'm on to the next. ___   ___

Outro

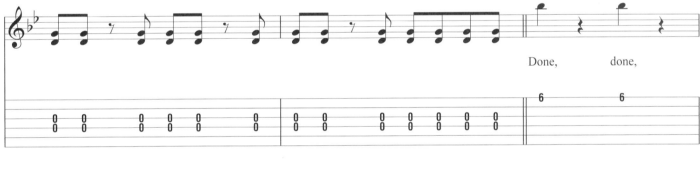

Done,   done,

on to the next ___ one. Done, ___ I'm done and I'm on to the next. ___

Additional Lyrics

2. Will I find a believer, another one who believes,
    Another one to deceive over and over down on my knees?
    If I get any closer and if you open up wide,
    And if you let me inside on and on I got nothing to hide.
    On and on I got nothing to hide.

Best of You

Words and Music by David Grohl, Christopher Shiflett, Oliver Taylor Hawkins and Nate Mendel

Strum Pattern: 1, 3
Pick Pattern: 2, 3

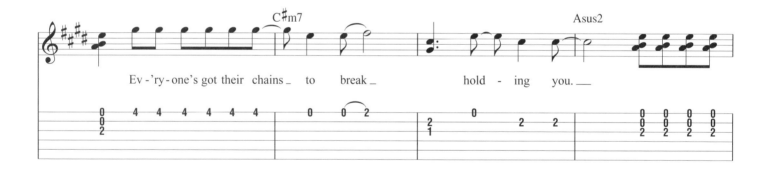

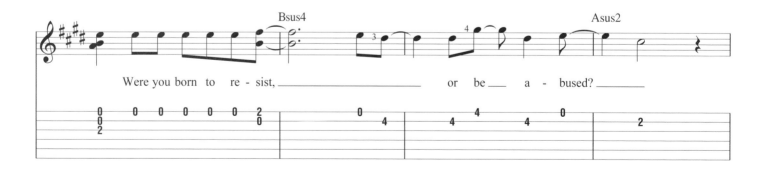

Chorus

Is some-one get-ting the best, ___ the best, ___ the best, ___ the best ___ of you? ___

Is someone get-ting the best, ___ the best, ___ the best, ___ the best ___ of you? ___

Are you gone ___ and on ___ to some - one new? ___

Verse

2. I need-ed some-where to hang ___ my head ___ with-out ___ your noose. _
___ a - gain. ___ but I ___ break loose. _

*Let chord ring.

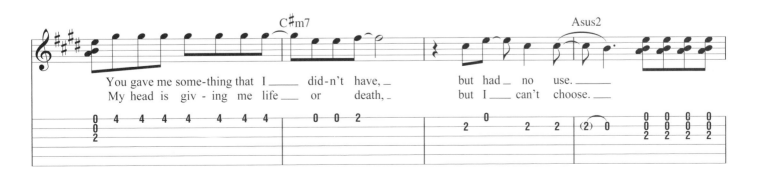

You gave me some-thing that I ___ did-n't have, _ but had ___ no use. ___
My head is giv - ing me life ___ or death, _ but I ___ can't choose. ___

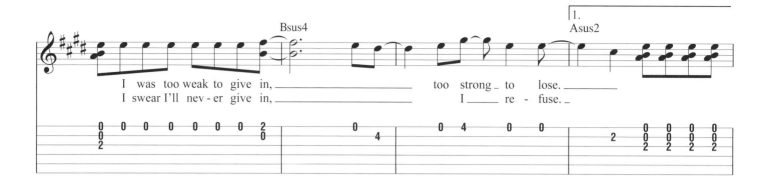

I was too weak to give in, _____ too strong _ to lose. _____
I swear I'll nev-er give in, _____ I _____ re - fuse. _____

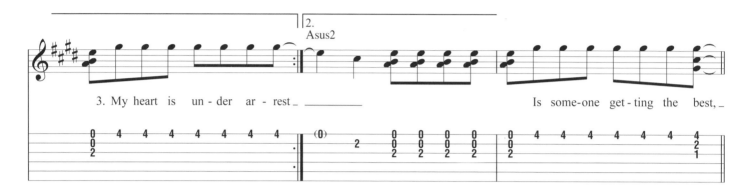

3. My heart is un-der ar-rest _____ Is some-one get-ting the best, _

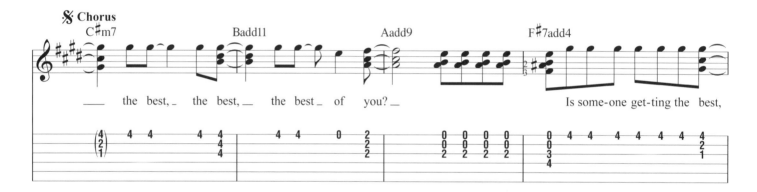

𝄋 Chorus

_____ the best, _ the best, _ the best _ of you? _ Is some-one get-ting the best,

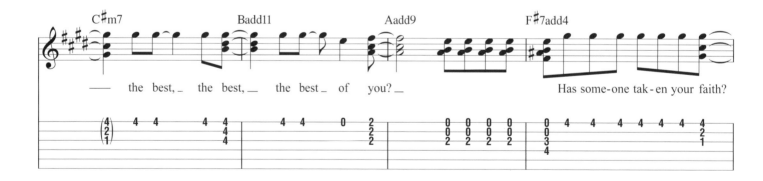

_____ the best, _ the best, _ the best _ of you? _ Has some-one tak-en your faith?

_____ It's real, _ the pain _ you feel. Your trust, _ you must _ con - fess. _ Is some-one get-ting the best,

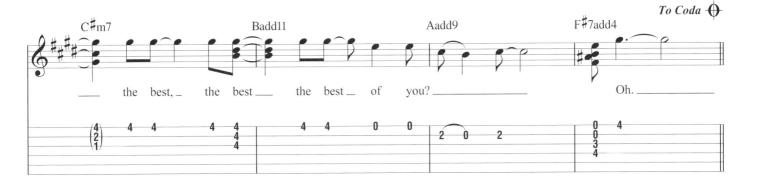

the best, __ the best __ the best __ of you? _____ Oh. _____

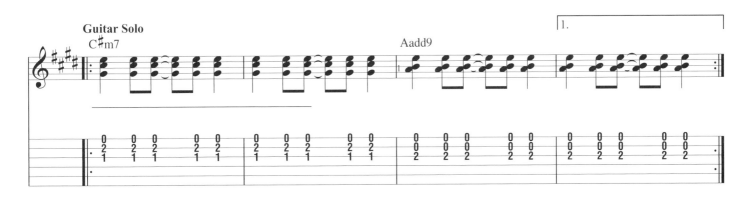

Guitar Solo

1.

2.

Oh, _____ oh. _____

1.

2.

oh. _____ Has some-one tak-en your faith? __ It's real, __ the pain

Chorus

__ you feel. _ The life, __ the love _ you thought _ you healed. _ The hope __ that stops _ the bro-

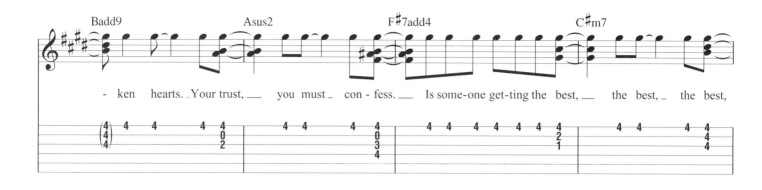

- ken hearts. Your trust, ___ you must _ con - fess. ___ Is some-one get-ting the best, ___ the best, _ the best,

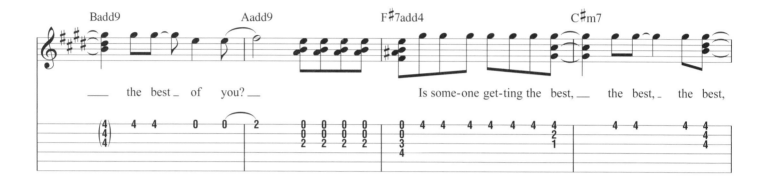

___ the best _ of you? ___ Is some-one get-ting the best, ___ the best, _ the best,

___ the best _ of you? _____ 4. I've got an-oth-er con-fes - sion my friend: _

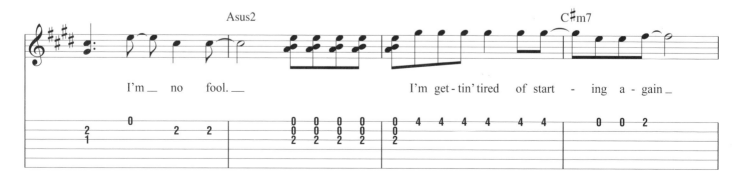

I'm _ no fool. __ I'm get-tin' tired of start - ing a-gain _

some - where new. ___

Were you born to re - sist, ___

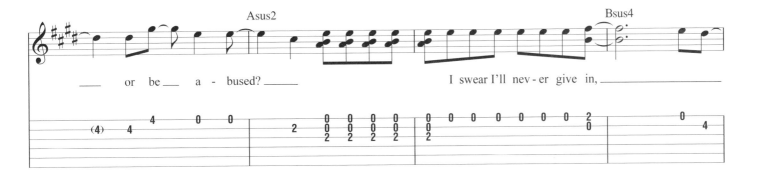

___ or be ___ a - bused? ___

I swear I'll nev - er give in, ___

D.S. al Coda

___ I ___ re - fuse. ___

Is some - one get - ting the best, ___

1., 2., 3. | 4.

Coda

Outro

*Vocal held 1st time only.

Big Me

Words and Music by David Grohl

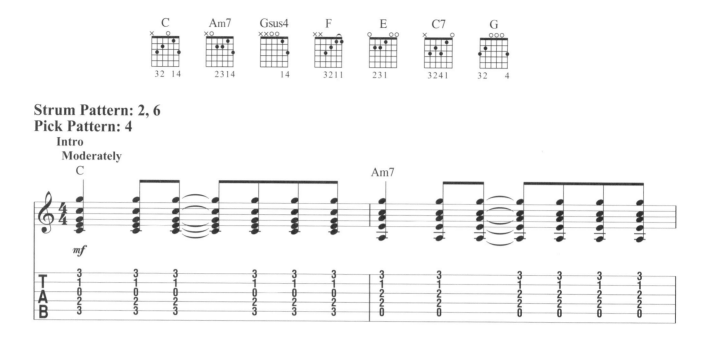

Strum Pattern: 2, 6
Pick Pattern: 4

Intro
Moderately

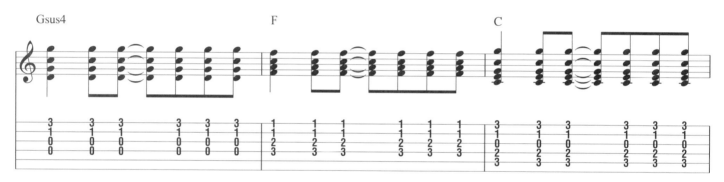

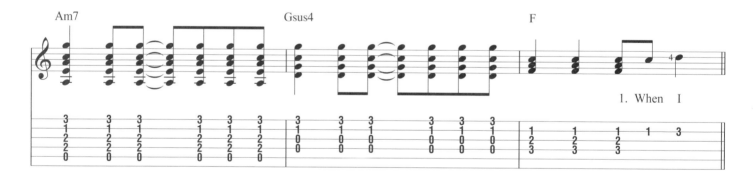

1. When I

Verse

talk a - bout it, car - ried on, rea - sons on - ly new. When I

2. *See additional lyrics*

Chorus

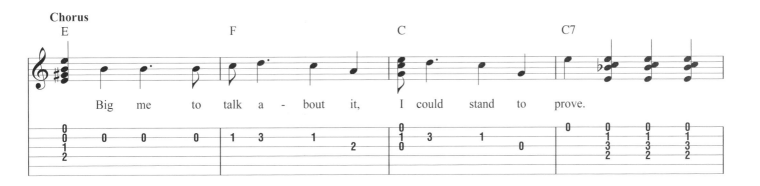

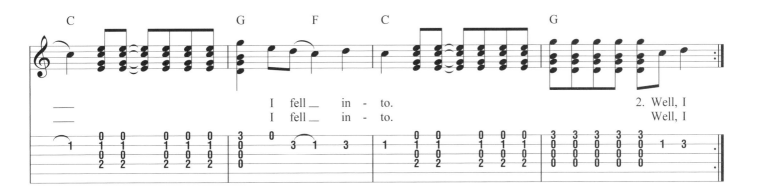

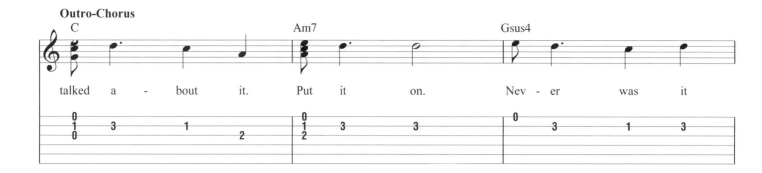

talked a - bout it. Put it on. Nev - er was it

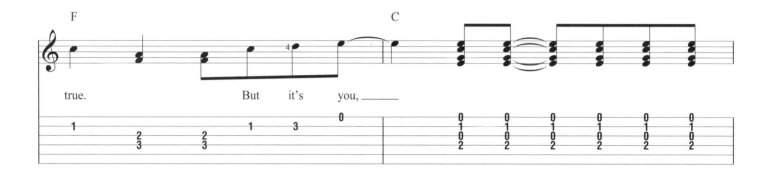

true. But it's you, _____

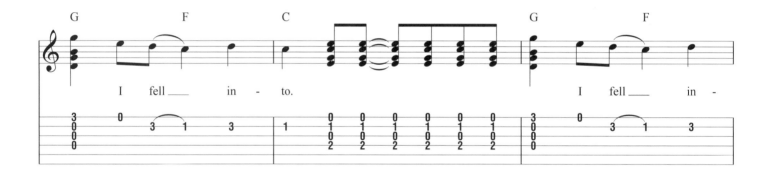

I fell _____ in - to. I fell _____ in -

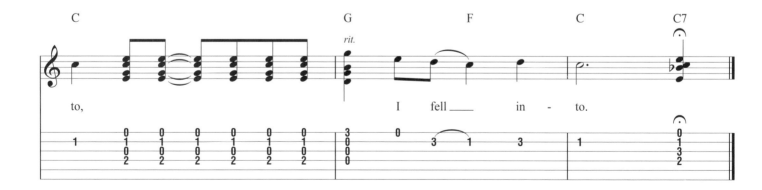

to, I fell _____ in - to.

Additional Lyrics

2. Well, I talked about it, carries on,
   Reasons only new.
   When I talk about it, Aries or
   Treasons all renew.

Monkey Wrench

Words and Music by David Grohl, Nate Mendel and Georg Ruthenberg

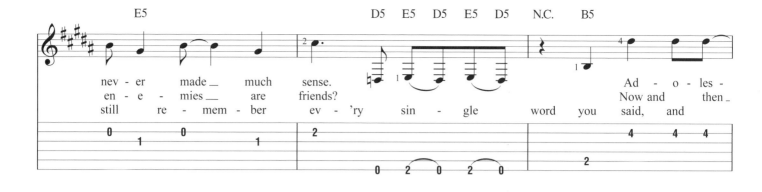

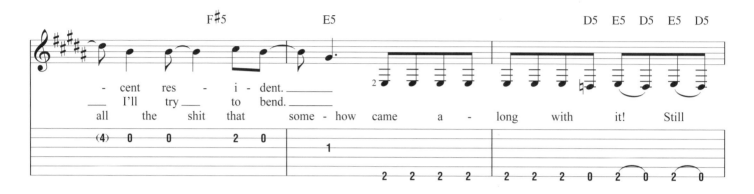

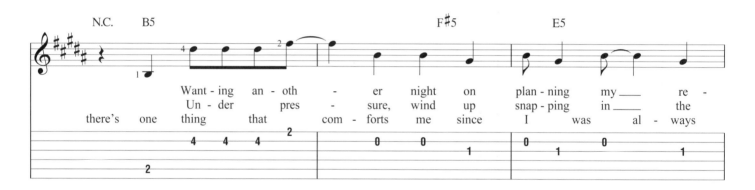

Pre-Chorus

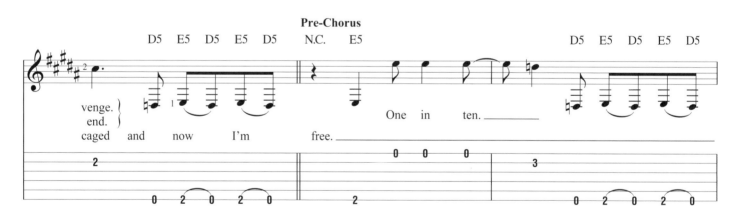

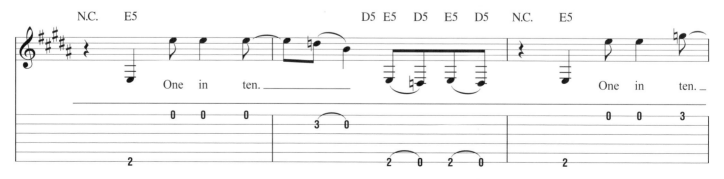

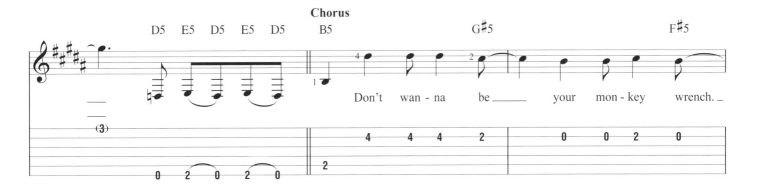

Chorus

Don't wan-na be _____ your mon-key wrench. _____

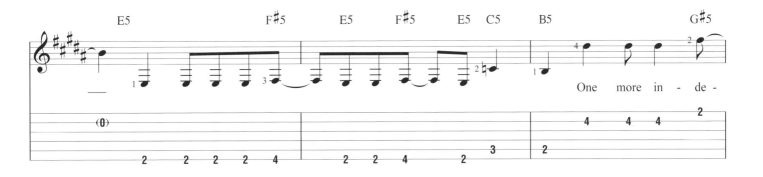

One more in-de-

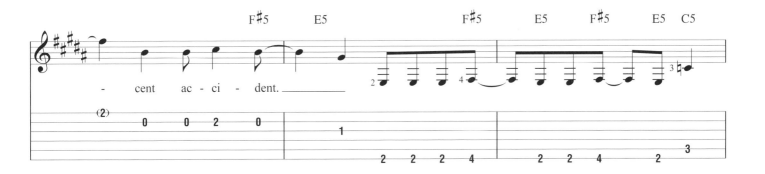

- cent ac-ci - dent. _____

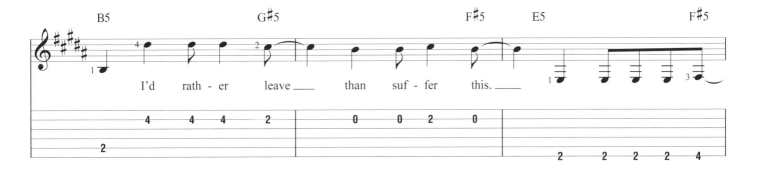

I'd rath-er leave ____ than suf-fer this. ____

I'll nev-er be _____ your mon-key wrench. _____

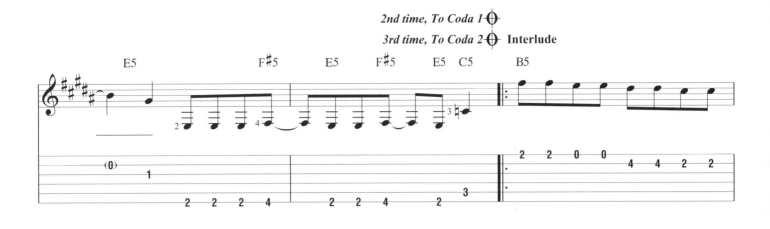

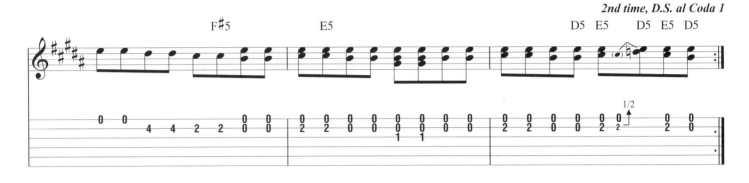

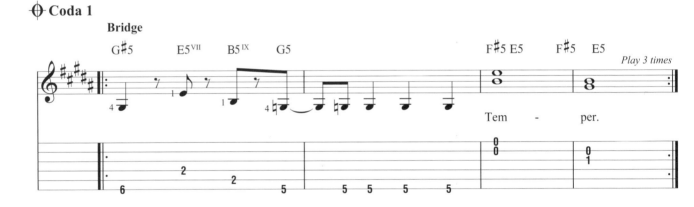

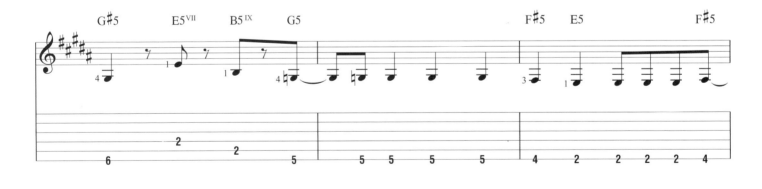

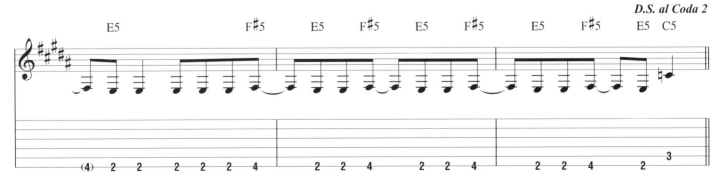

Coda 2
Outro

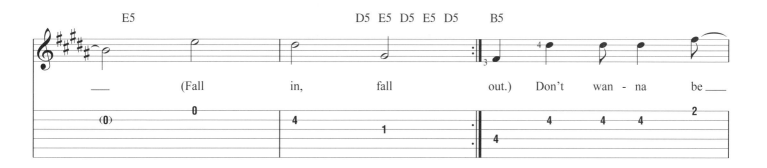

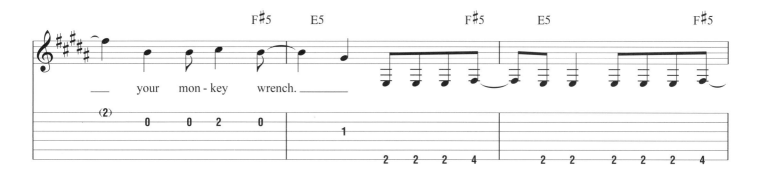

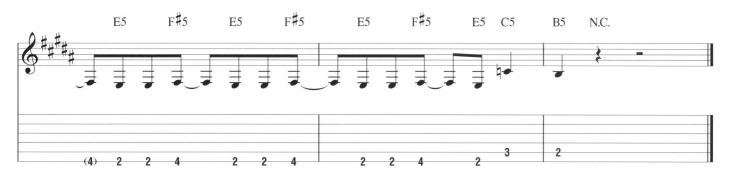

Everlong

Words and Music by David Grohl

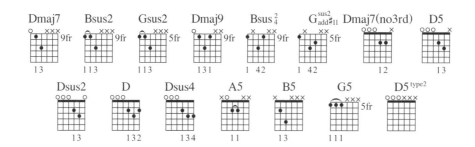

Drop D tuning:
(low to high) D-A-D-G-B-E

Strum Pattern: 1
Pick Pattern: 4

Intro
Moderate Rock

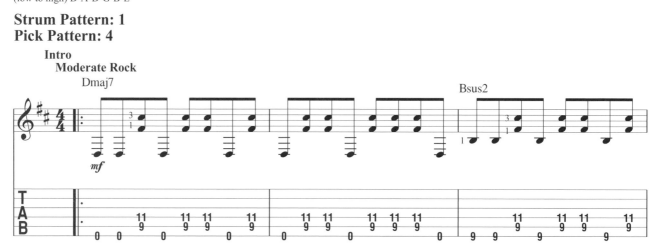

𝄋 Interlude

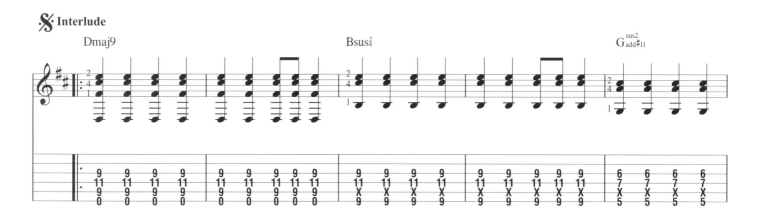

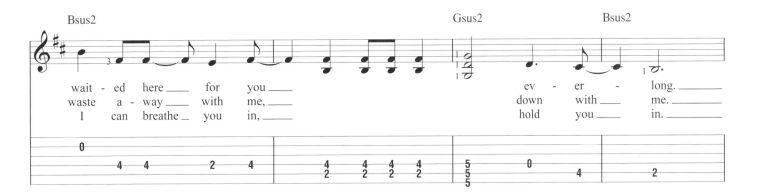

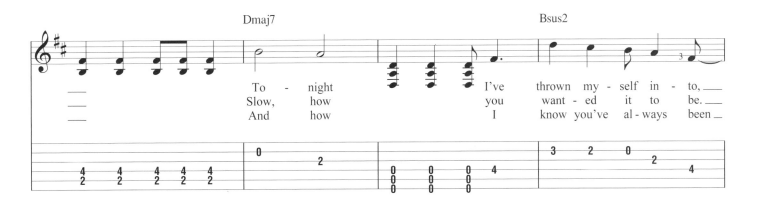

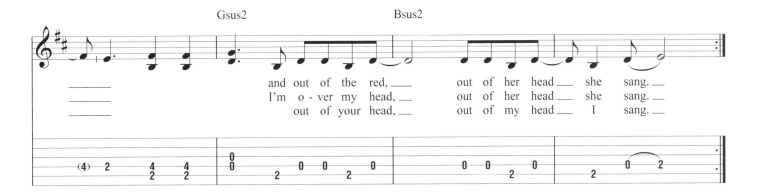

Pre-Chorus

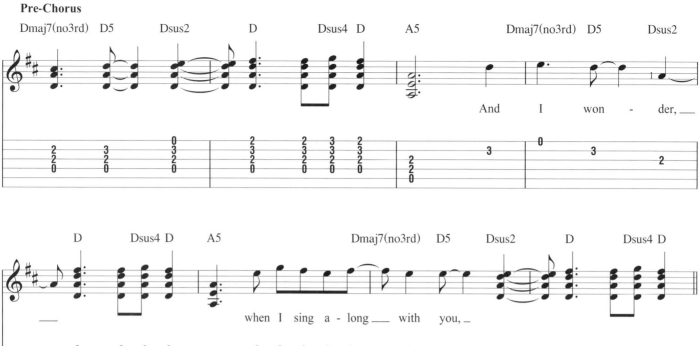

𝄋𝄋 Chorus

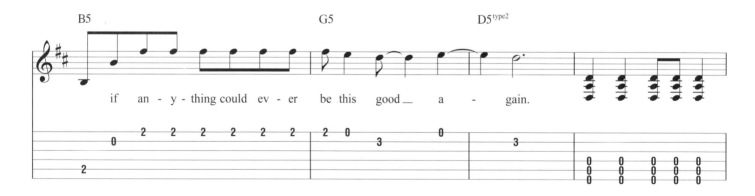

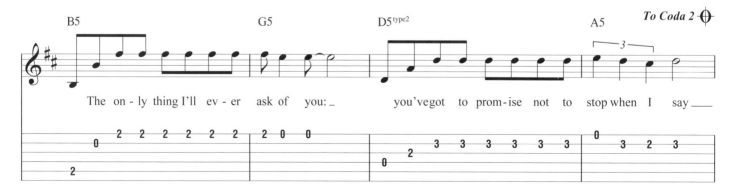

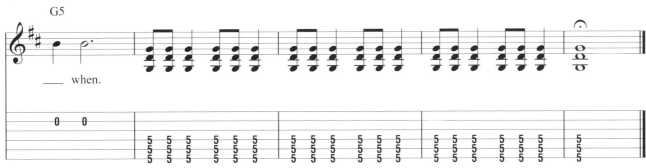

I'll Stick Around

Words and Music by David Grohl

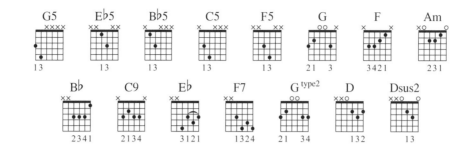

Strum Pattern: 1

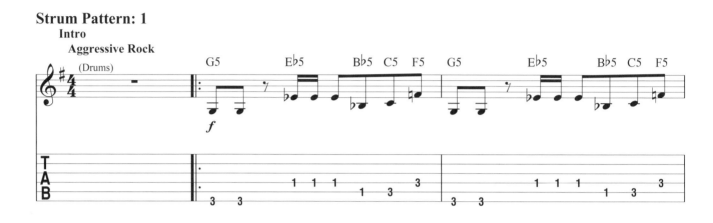

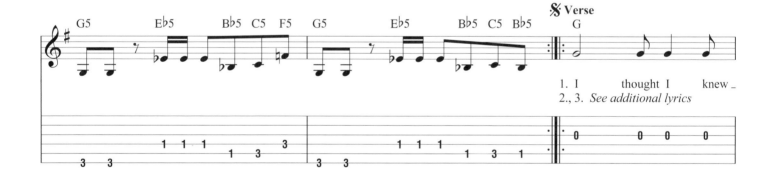

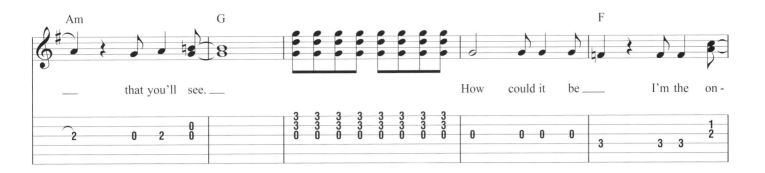

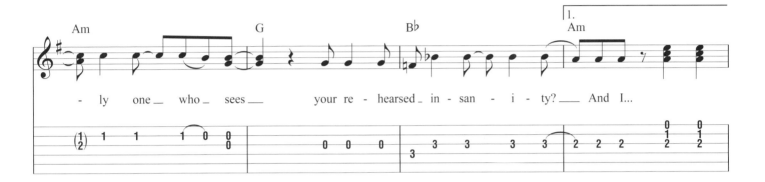

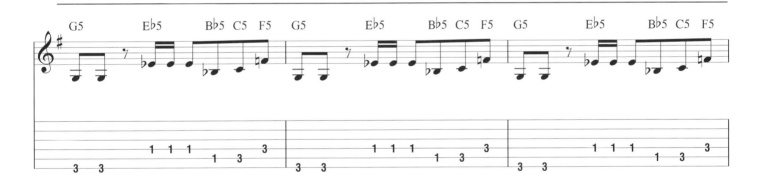

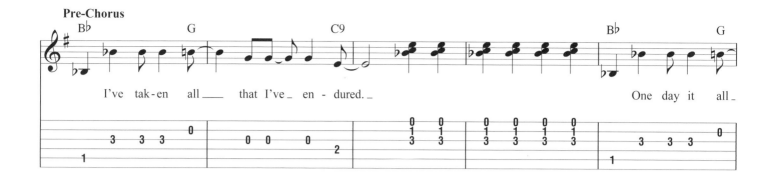

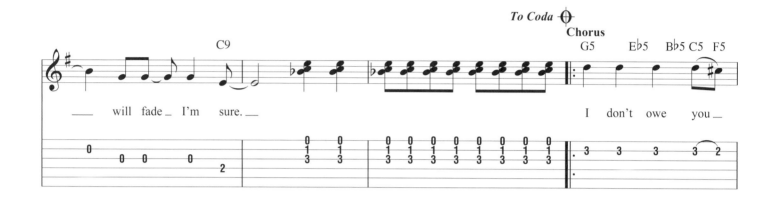

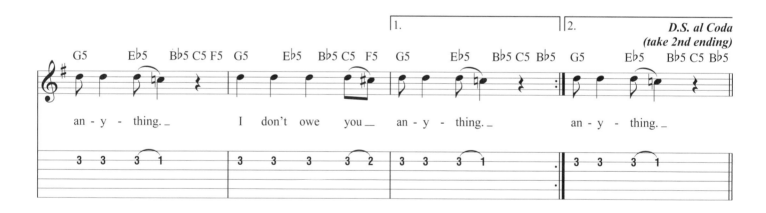

*Tie into beat 1
on repeats.

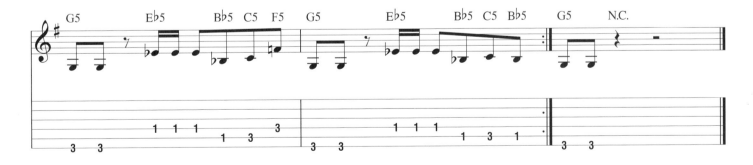

Additional Lyrics

2. I still refuse all the methods you abuse.
   It's alright if you're confused, let me be.
   I've been around all the pawns you've gagged and bound.
   They'll come back and knock you down and I'll be free.

3. I had no hand in your ever desperate plan.
   It returns and when it lands words are due.
   I should have known we were better off alone.
   I looked in and I was shown you were too.

Learn to Fly

Words and Music by David Grohl, Oliver Taylor Hawkins and Nate Mendel

sat a-round laugh-ing and watched the last one die. ___ I'm

§ § Chorus

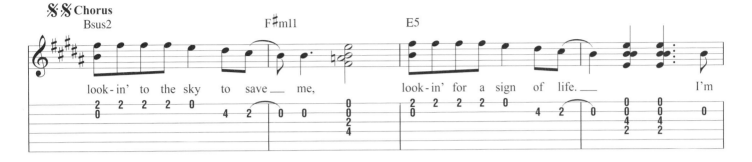

look-in' to the sky to save ___ me, look-in' for a sign of life. ___ I'm

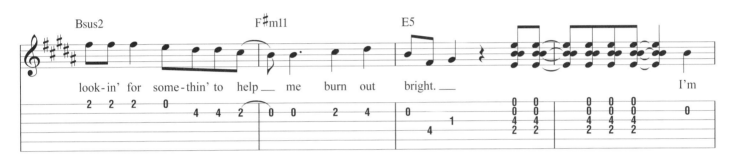

look-in' for some-thin' to help ___ me burn out bright. ___ I'm

look-in' for a com-pli-ca-tion, look-in' 'cause I'm tired of { ly-
                                                                 try-

To Coda 1 ⊕
To Coda 2 ⊕

in.' }
in.' }
Make my way back home when I learn to fly ___

Interlude

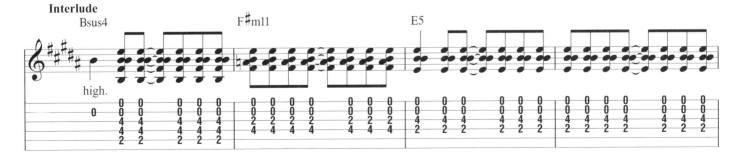

high.

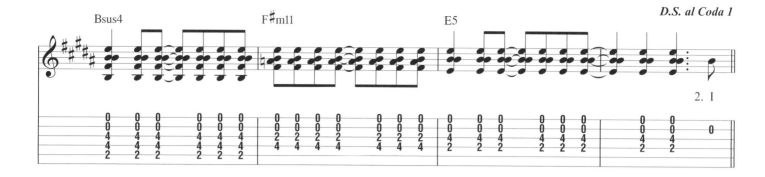

Coda 1

home when I learn to fly __ high. Make my way back home when I learn to...

Bridge

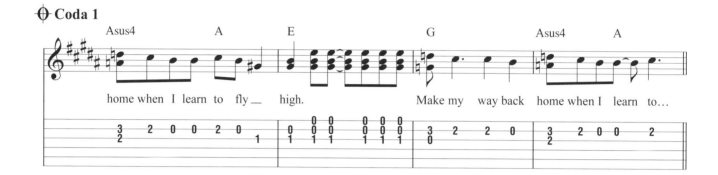

Fly a - long with me, __ I can't quite make __ it a - lone. _____

Try to make __ this life my own. _____ life my own. __ I'm __

Coda 2

Outro-Chorus

home when I learn __ to... look - in' to the sky to save __ me,

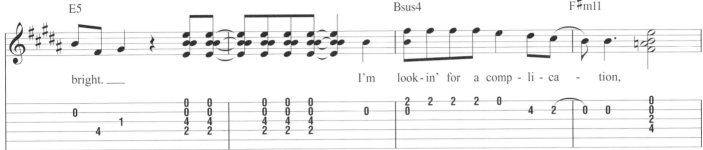

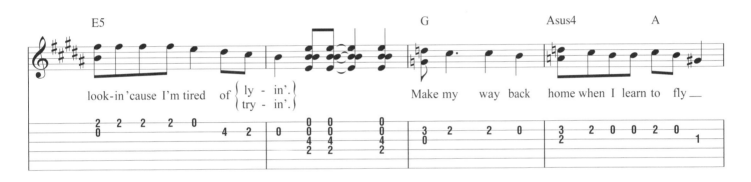

Additional Lyrics

2. I think I'm dyin' missing patience,
   It can wait one night.
   Give it all away if you give me one last try.
   We'll live happily ever trapped
   If you just save my life.
   Runnin' down the angels and ev'rything's all right.

Long Road to Ruin

Words and Music by David Grohl, Christopher Shiflett, Oliver Taylor Hawkins and Nate Mendel

C   Fsus2   F/A   Gadd4/B   F/C   D

F   G/B   Am   Fadd9   C5   Am7

Strum Pattern: 1
Pick Pattern: 1

Verse
Moderately fast

*C

mf

1. Hey now, _ don't make a sound. Say, have _ you heard the news _ to-
2. Let's say _ we take this town. No king _ or queen of an - y

Chord symbols reflect basic harmony.

Fsus2

day? One _ flag was _ tak - en down _____ to raise _ an - oth - er in its
state. Get _ up to _ shut it down. _____ O - pen _ the streets and raise the

C

place. A heav - y cross _ you bear, a stub - born heart re - mains _ un -
gates. I know a wall _ to scale. I know _ a fear with - out _ a

Fsus2

changed. No home, _ no life, _____ no love, _ no stran - ger sing - ing in your
name. Head on _____ with - out _____ a care _ be - fore _ it's way too late. It*

*2nd time, skip to **Pre-Chorus**.

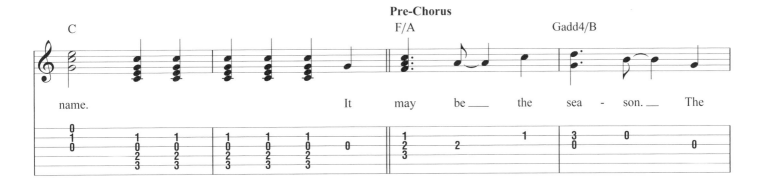

C

name. It may be ___ the sea - son. ___ The

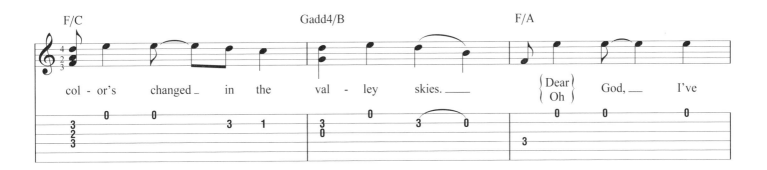

F/C   Gadd4/B   F/A

col - or's changed ___ in the val - ley skies. ___ { Dear / Oh } God, ___ I've

Gadd4/B   F/C   D

sealed my fate. Run - ning through hell, heav - en can wait.

% Chorus

F   C   F   C   G/B

Long road to ru - in there in your eyes, un - der the cold street - lights.

1.

Am   D   Fadd9

No to - mor - row. No dead end ___ in sight. ___

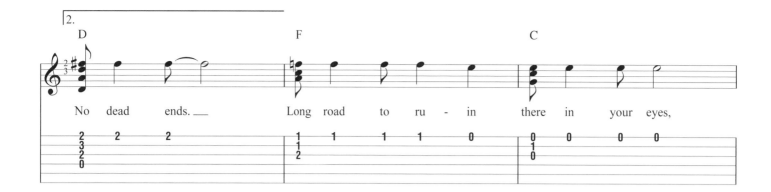

No dead ends. ___ Long road to ru - in there in your eyes,

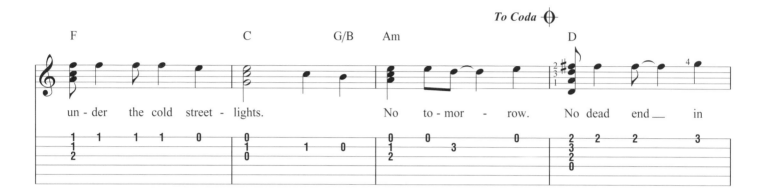

To Coda

un - der the cold street - lights. No to - mor - row. No dead end ___ in

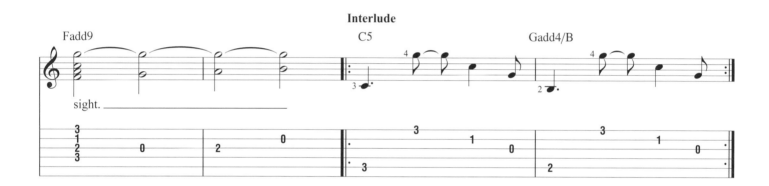

Interlude

sight. _____

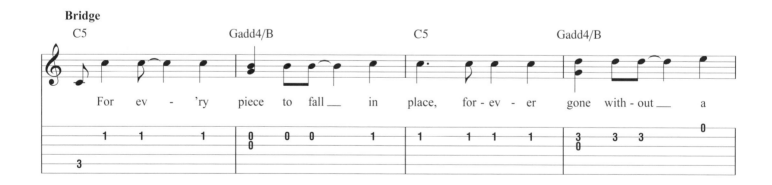

Bridge

For ev - 'ry piece to fall ___ in place, for - ev - er gone with - out ___ a

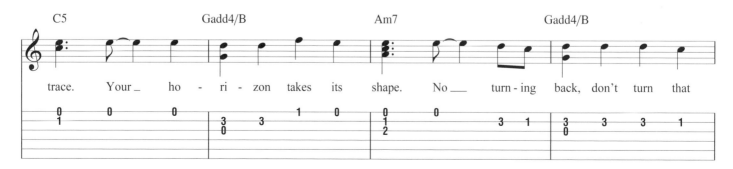

trace. Your ___ ho - ri - zon takes its shape. No ___ turn - ing back, don't turn that

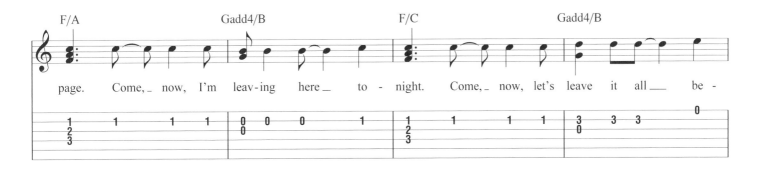

D.S. al Coda
(take 2nd ending)

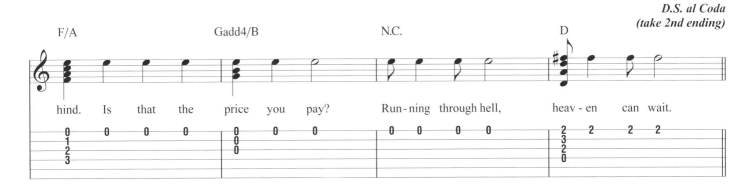

Coda

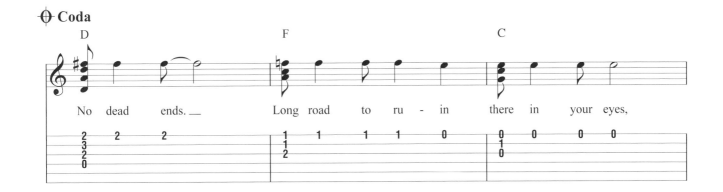

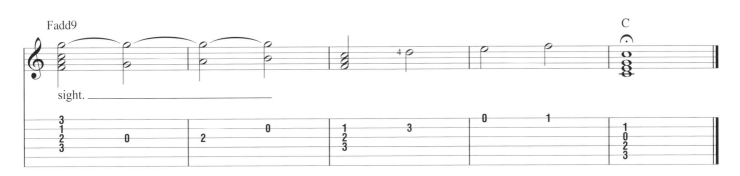

My Hero

Words and Music by David Grohl, Nate Mendel and Georg Ruthenberg

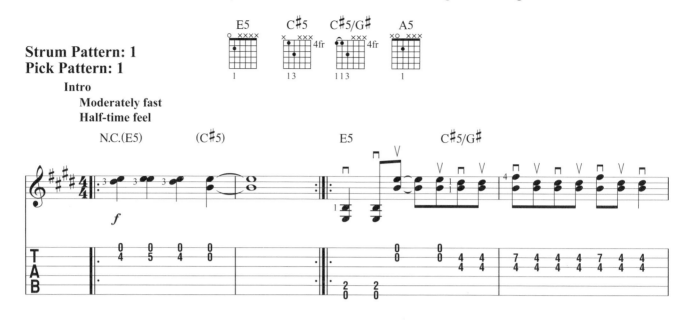

Strum Pattern: 1
Pick Pattern: 1

Intro
Moderately fast
Half-time feel

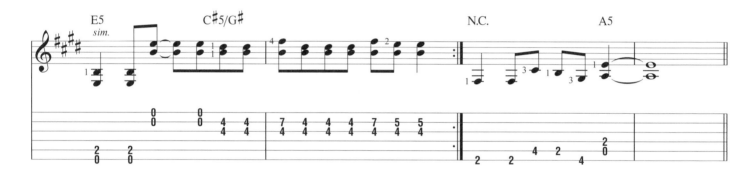

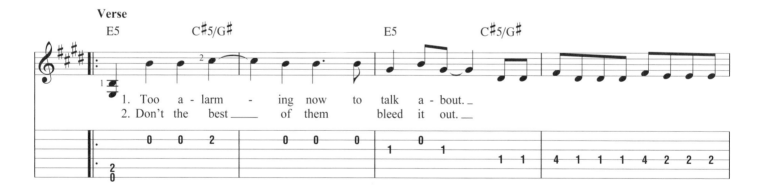

Verse

1. Too a - larm - ing now to talk a - bout. _
2. Don't the best ___ of them bleed it out. _

Take your pic - tures down and shake it out. _
while the rest ___ of them pe - ter out? _

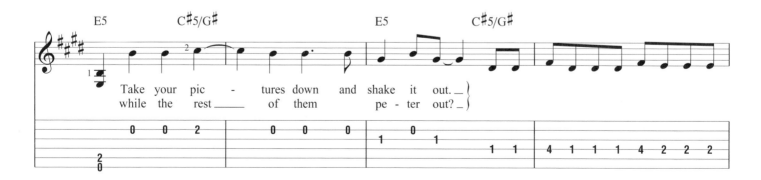

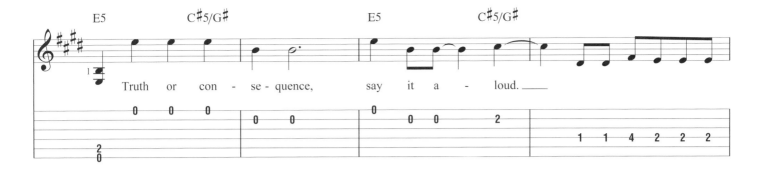

Truth or con - se - quence, say it a - loud. ____

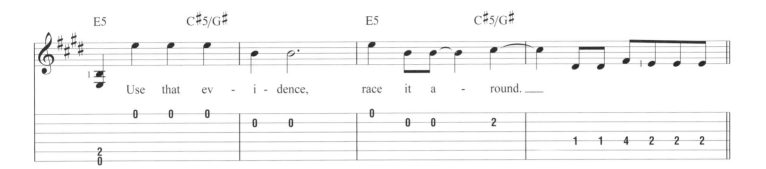

Use that ev - i - dence, race it a - round. ____

𝄋 Chorus

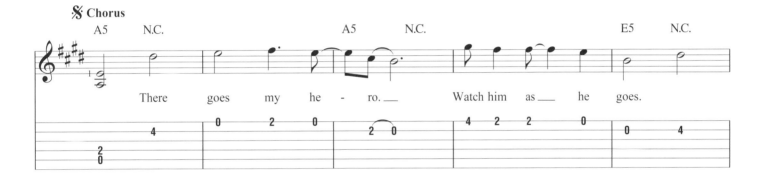

There goes my he - ro. ____ Watch him as ____ he goes.

There goes my he -

3rd time, To Coda ⊕

- ro. ____ He's or - di - nar - y.

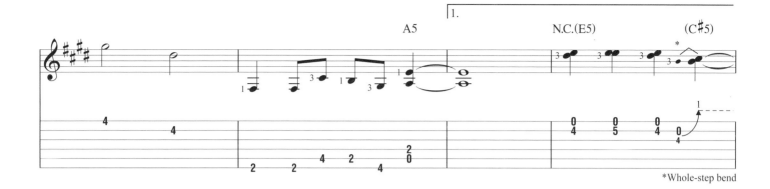

*Whole-step bend

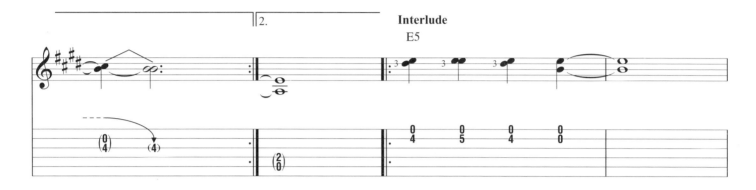

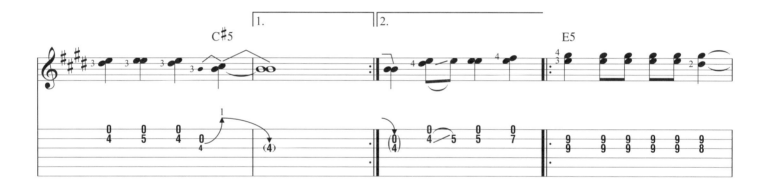

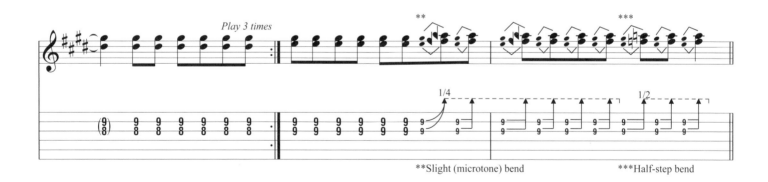

**Slight (microtone) bend   ***Half-step bend

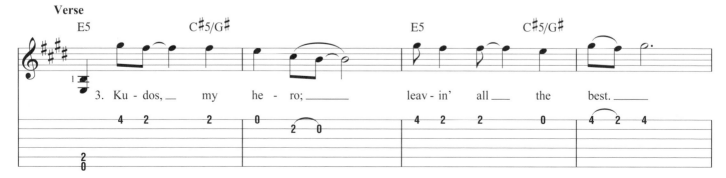

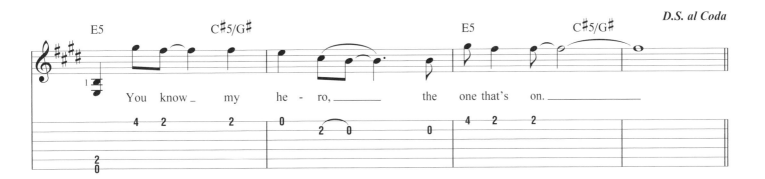

Coda

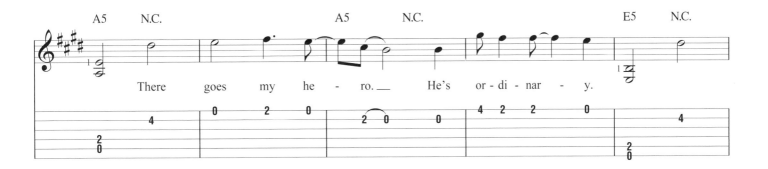

The Pretender

Words and Music by David Grohl, Christopher Shiflett, Oliver Taylor Hawkins and Nate Mendel

Strum Pattern: 1
Pick Pattern: 1

Intro
Fast
Half-time feel

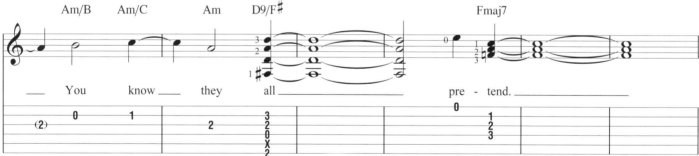

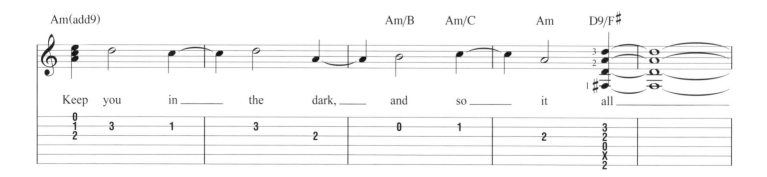

Interlude
End half-time feel

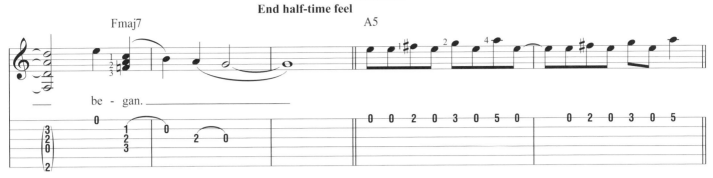

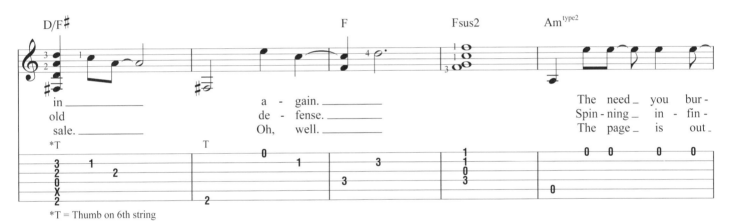

*T = Thumb on 6th string

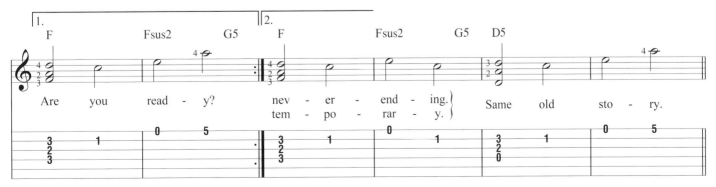

%.%. **Chorus**

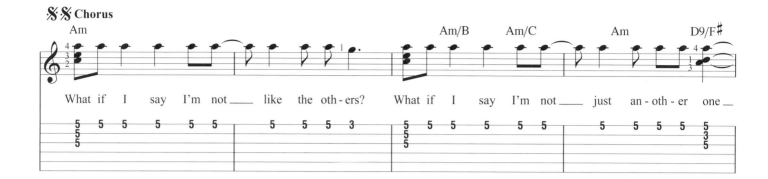

What if I say I'm not ___ like the oth-ers? What if I say I'm not ___ just an-oth-er one ___

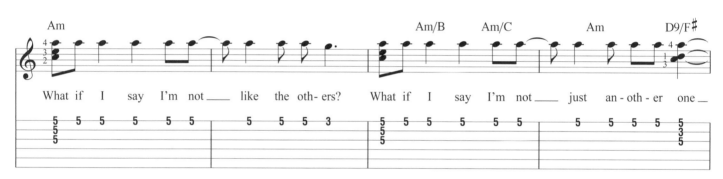

___ of your plays? You're the pre-tend - er. What if I say I will nev-er sur-ren - der?

What if I say I'm not ___ like the oth-ers? What if I say I'm not ___ just an-oth-er one ___

2nd time, To Coda 1

3rd time, To Coda 2

4th time, To Coda 3

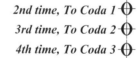

___ of your plays? You're the pre-tend - er. What if I say I will nev-er sur-ren - der?

Interlude

A5

D.S. al Coda 1
(take 2nd ending)

Coda 1

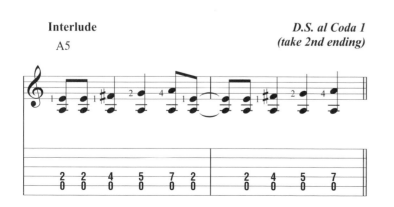

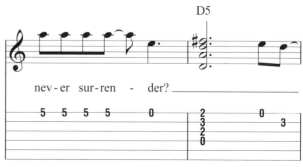

nev-er sur-ren - der? _____

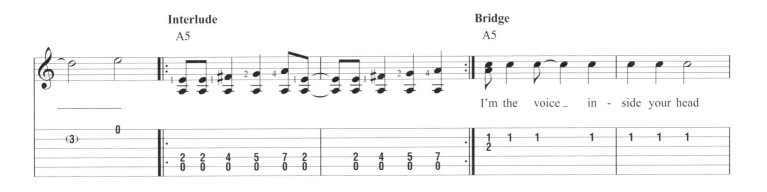

Interlude
A5

Bridge
A5

I'm the voice _ in - side your head

you re - fuse _ to hear. I'm the face that you have to face, mir-rored in ___ your

stare. I'm what's left. _ I'm what's right. _ I'm the en - e - my. ___

I'm the hand that will take you down, bring you to ___ your knees. So who ___ are you? _

___ Yeah, who ___ are you? ___ Yeah, who ___ are you? ___ Yeah,

Verse
Half-time feel
w/ Intro pattern

who ___ are you? ___ 5. Keep you in ___ the dark. ___ You know _

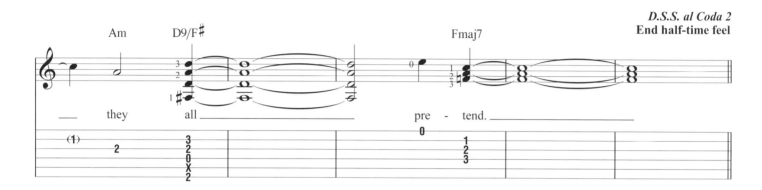

D.S.S. al Coda 2
End half-time feel

___ they all _____ pre - tend. _____

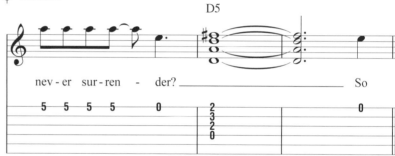

Coda 2   *D.S.S. al Coda 3*   **Coda 3**

nev - er sur - ren - der?   nev - er sur - ren - der? _____ So

Outro

who ___ are you? ___ Yeah, who ___ are you? ___ Yeah,

who ___ are you? ___

Shame Shame

Words and Music by David Grohl, Christopher Shiflett, Oliver Taylor Hawkins,
Rami Jaffee, Nate Mendel and Georg Ruthenberg

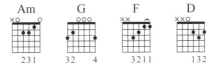

Strum Pattern: 4, 6
Pick Pattern: 5, 6

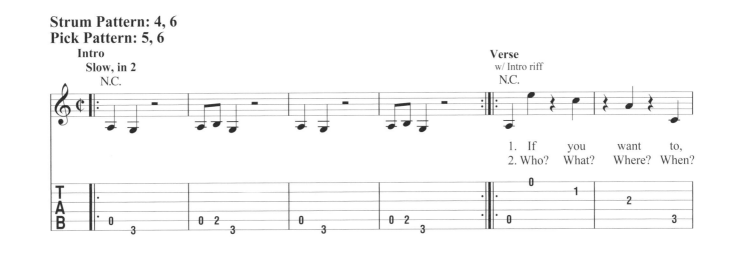

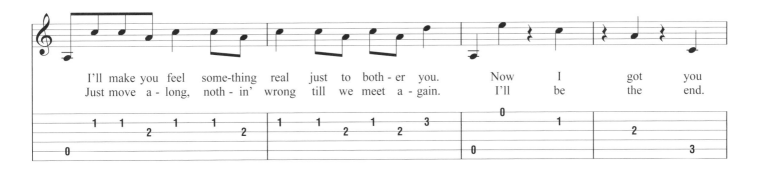

moon, be the sun, be the rain in your song. Go and put that rec-ord on. If you

Play 1st time only

Pre-Chorus
N.C.

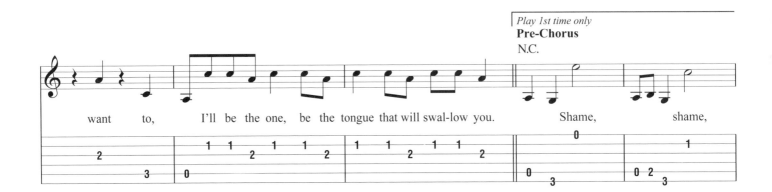

want to, I'll be the one, be the tongue that will swal-low you. Shame, shame,

shame, shame. Shame, shame, shame, shame.

Chorus

Am   G   F   D

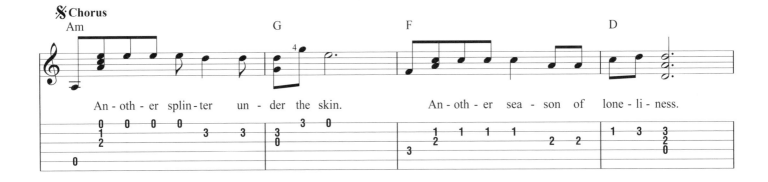

An - oth - er splin - ter un - der the skin. An - oth - er sea - son of lone - li - ness.

Am   G   F   D

I found a rea - son and bur - ied it be - neath a moun - tain of emp - ti - ness. Oh. _____

Interlude

3rd time, To Coda ⊕

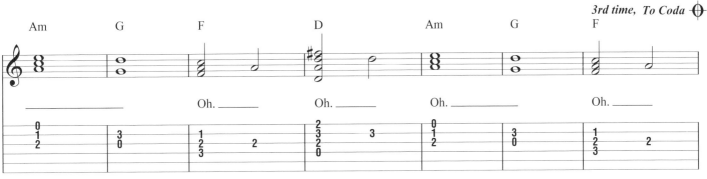

Oh. _____ Oh. _____ Oh. _____ Oh. _____ Oh. _____

1.

Oh. Shame, shame, shame, shame.

2nd time, D.S. al Coda

Oh. _____ Shame, shame, shame, shame.

⊕ **Coda**

Outro
N.C.

Shame, shame,

shame, shame. Shame, shame, shame, shame.

Rope

Words and Music by David Grohl, Christopher Shiflett, Oliver Taylor Hawkins, Nate Mendel and Georg Ruthenberg

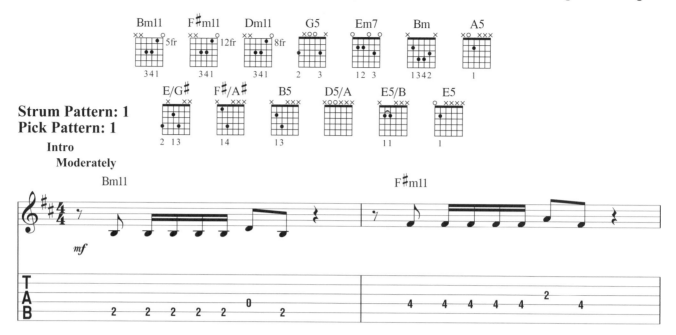

Strum Pattern: 1
Pick Pattern: 1

Intro
Moderately

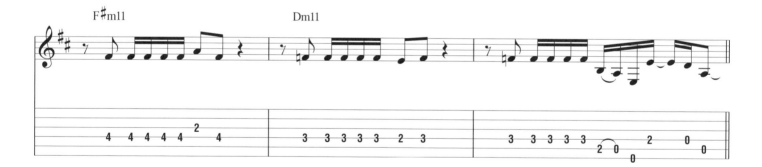

Verse

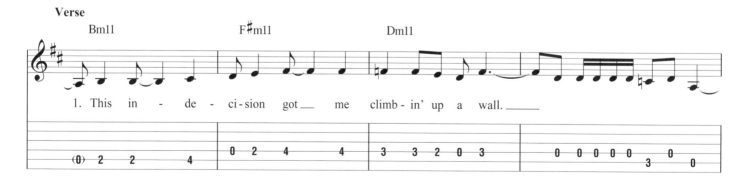

1. This in- de- ci- sion got ___ me climb- in' up a wall. ___

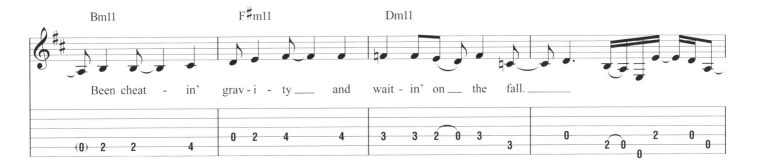

Been cheat - in' grav-i-ty ___ and wait-in' on ___ the fall. ___

How did this ___ come o - ver me? ___ Thought I was a - bove ___ it all. ___

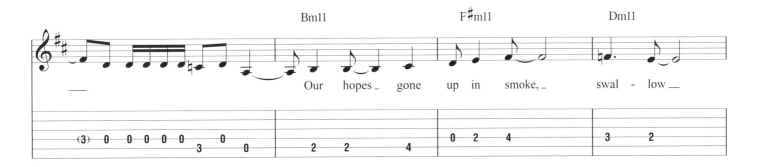

___ Our hopes ___ gone up in smoke, ___ swal - low ___

𝄋 Pre-Chorus

your crown. ___ *Shouted: Yow!* On a ___

___ kiss, ___ thought I'd save ___ my breath ___ for you. *Shouted: Yow!*

On a _____ kiss, _____ thought I'd save _____ my breath _____ for

Chorus

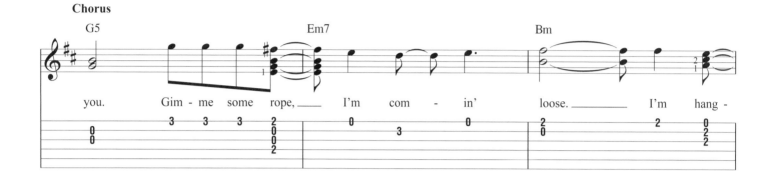

you. Gim - me some rope, _____ I'm com - in' loose. _____ I'm hang -

- in' on _____ you. Gim - me some rope, _____ I'm com - in'

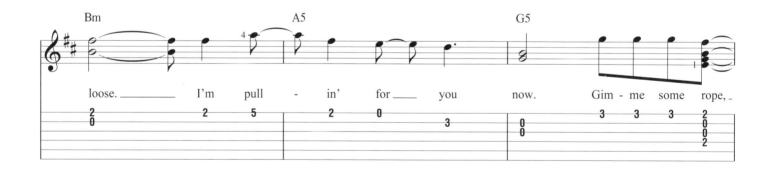

loose. _____ I'm pull - in' for _____ you now. Gim - me some rope,

_____ I'm com - in' out of my head, _____ in - to the clear. _____ When

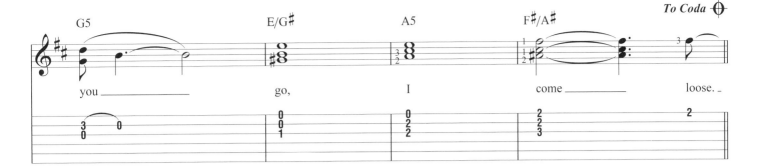

you _____ go, I come _____ loose.

Interlude

Verse

2. These prem - o -

ni-tions got _ me cry-in' up a storm. _____ Leave your _ con -

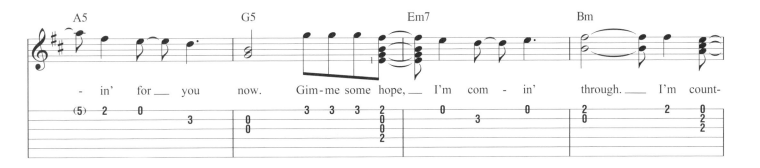

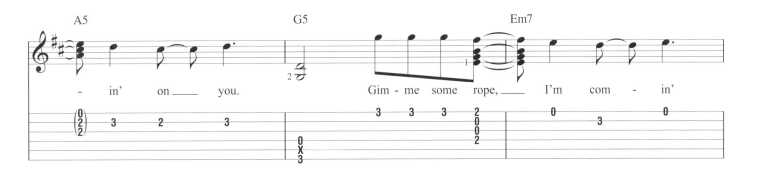

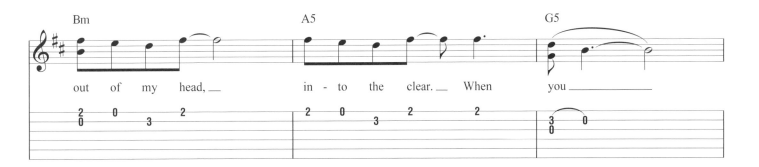

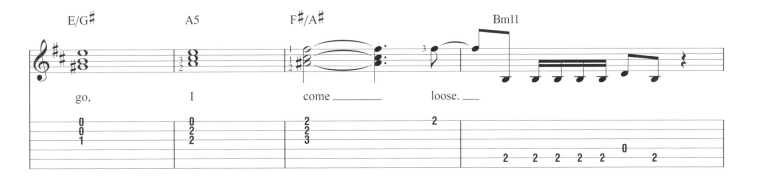

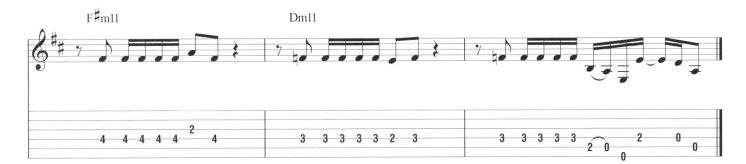

These Days

Words and Music by David Grohl, Christopher Shiflett, Oliver Taylor Hawkins, Nate Mendel and Georg Ruthenberg

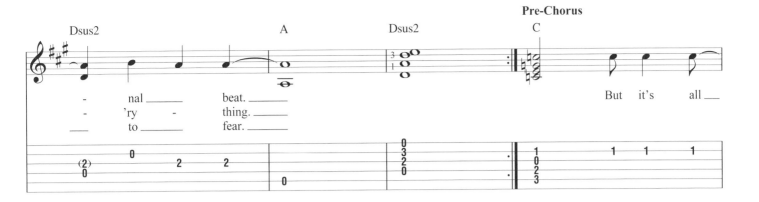

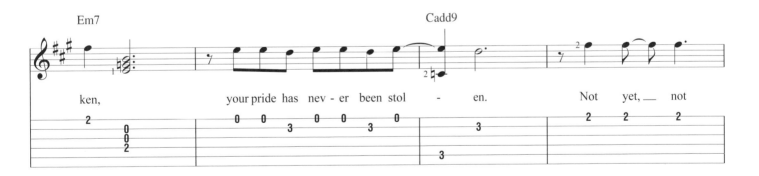

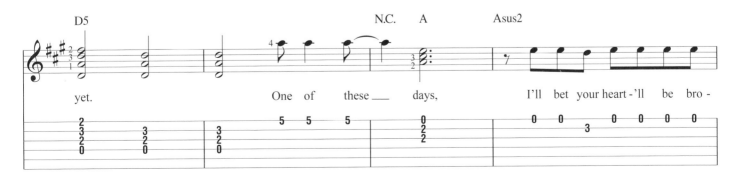

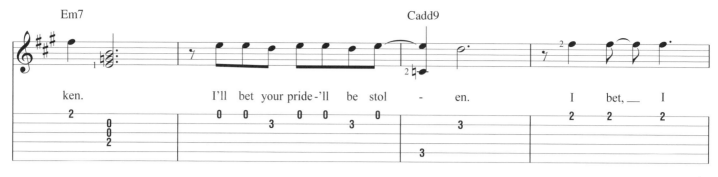

ken. I'll bet your pride -'ll be stol - en. I bet, ___ I

2nd time, To Coda 1 ⊕

3rd time, To Coda 2 ⊕

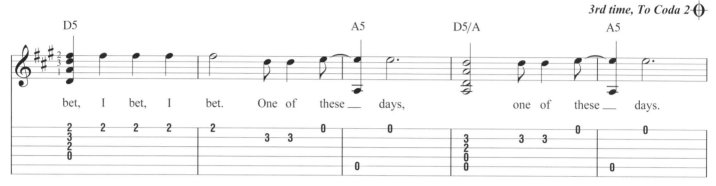

bet, I bet, I bet. One of these ___ days, one of these ___ days.

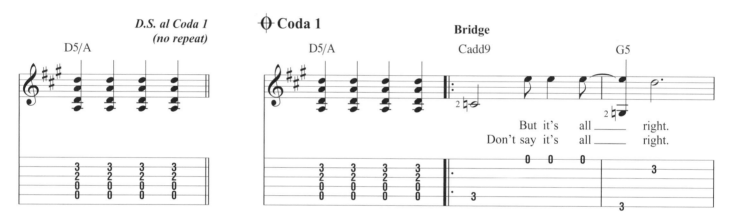

D.S. al Coda 1
(no repeat)

⊕ **Coda 1**

Bridge

But it's all _____ right.
Don't say it's all _____ right.

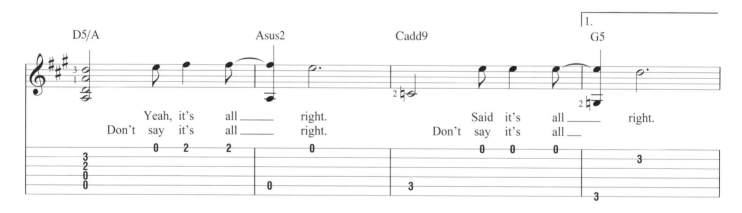

1.

Yeah, it's all _____ right.
Don't say it's all _____ right.

Said it's all _____ right.
Don't say it's all ___

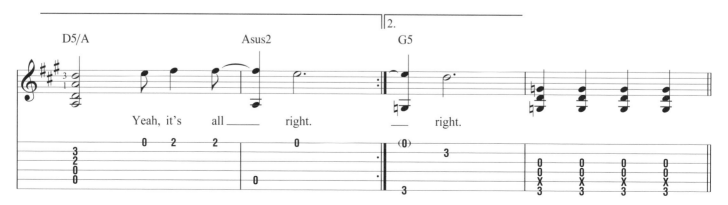

2.

Yeah, it's all _____ right. ___ right.

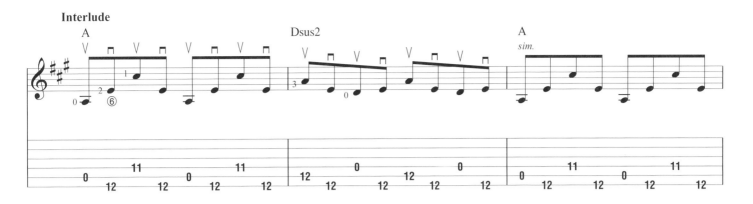

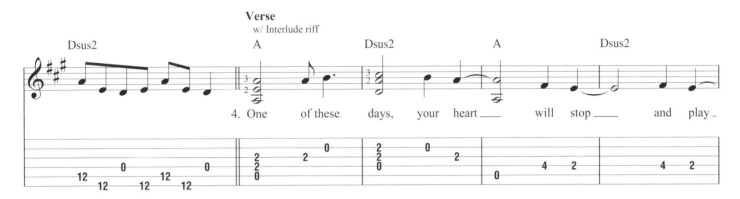

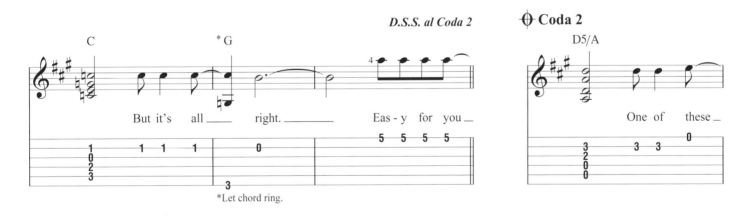

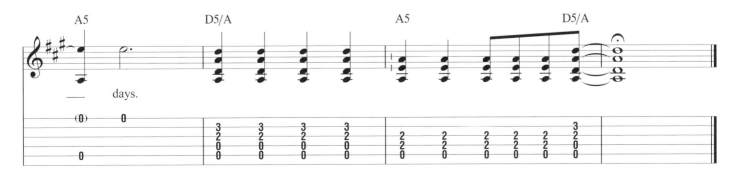

Times Like These

Words and Music by David Grohl, Christopher Shiflett, Oliver Taylor Hawkins and Nate Mendel

Strum Pattern: 1
Pick Pattern: 1

Intro
Moderately fast

*Chord symbols reflect combined harmony.

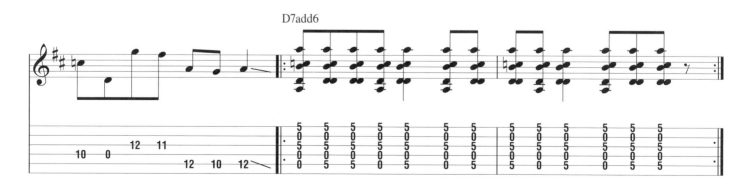

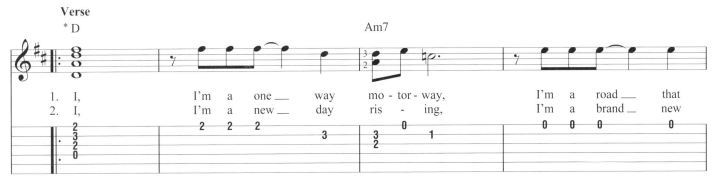

*Chord symbols reflect implied harmony.

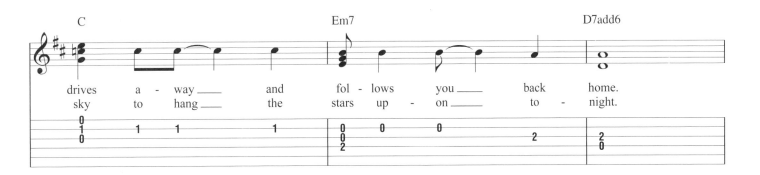

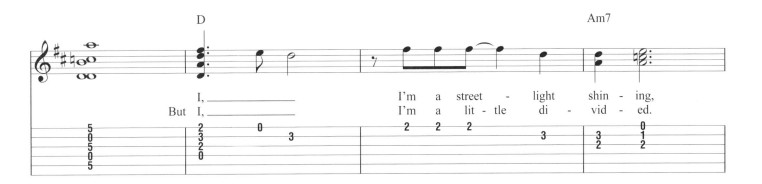

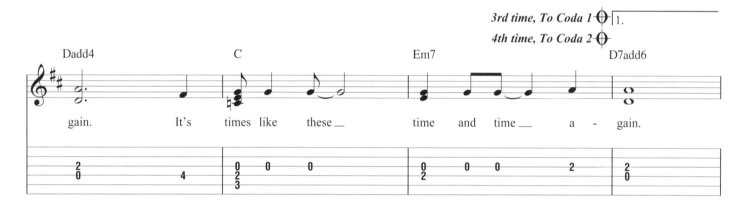

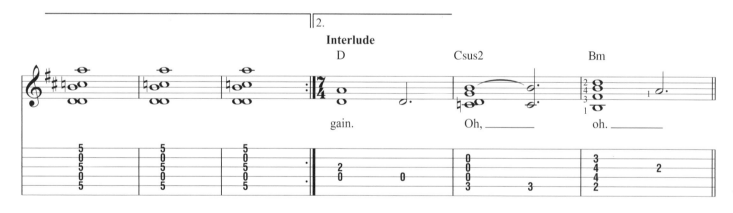

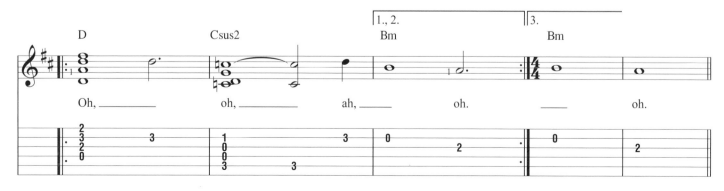

Coda 1

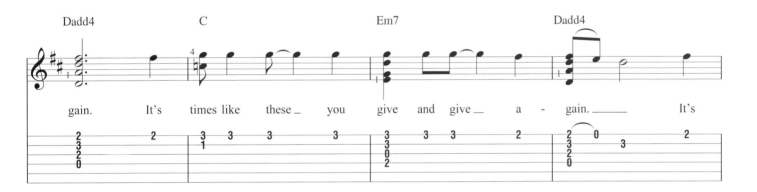

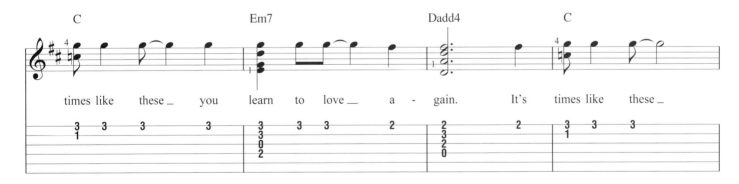

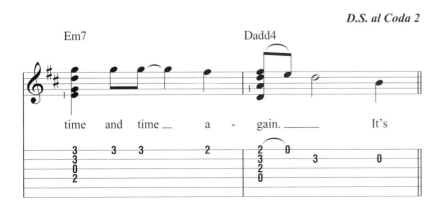

This Is a Call

Words and Music by David Grohl

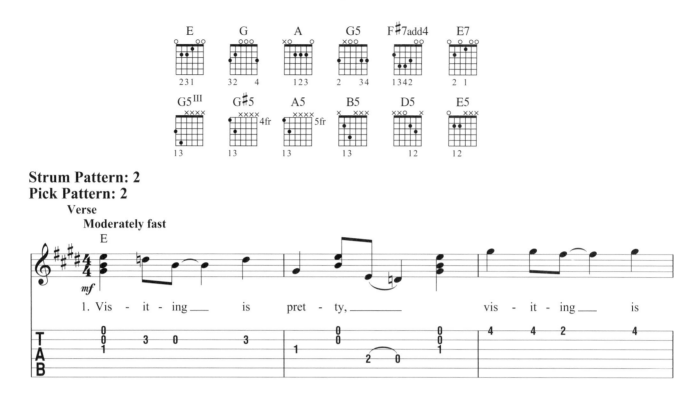

Strum Pattern: 2
Pick Pattern: 2

Verse
Moderately fast

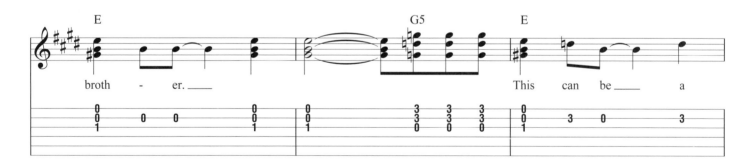

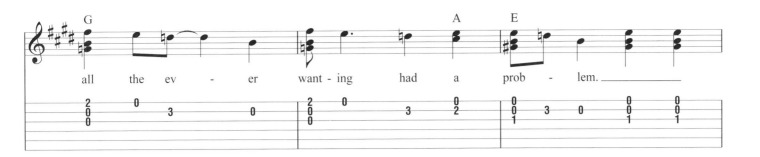

all the ev - er want - ing had a prob - lem.

Chorus

This is a call ___ to all ___ my

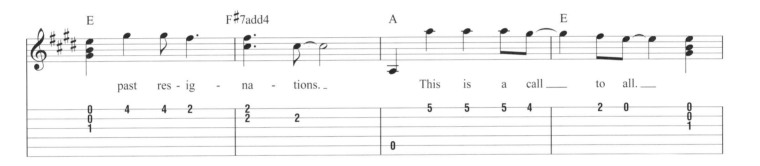

past res - ig - na - tions. ___ This is a call ___ to all. ___

Verse

2., 4. Fing - er - nails ___ are pret - ty, ___
3. *See additional lyrics*

fing - er - nails ___ are good. ___ Seems that all they ev - er

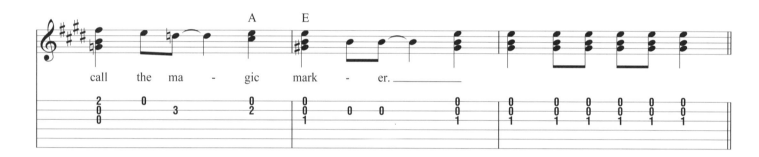

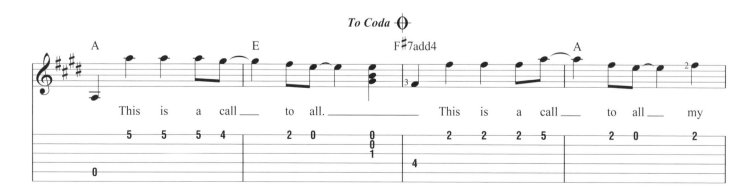

past res - ig - na - tions. _____ It's been too long. _____

Interlude

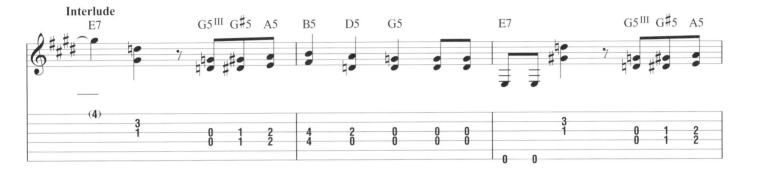

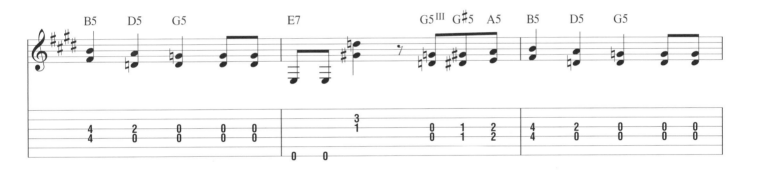

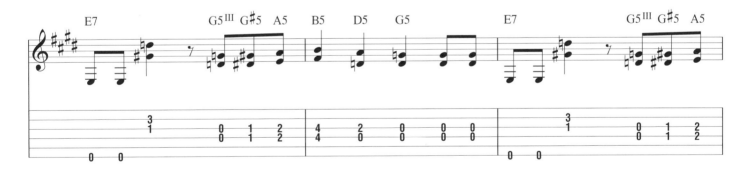

2nd time, D.S. al Coda

1., 2.

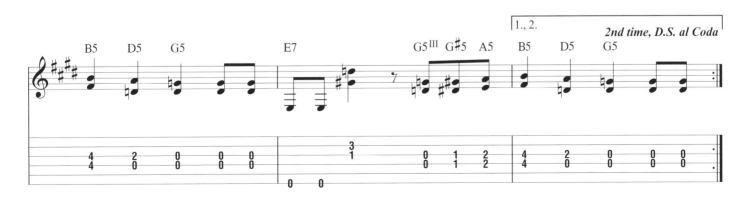

Coda

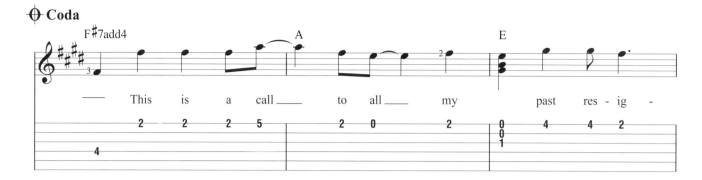

This is a call ___ to all ___ my past res - ig -

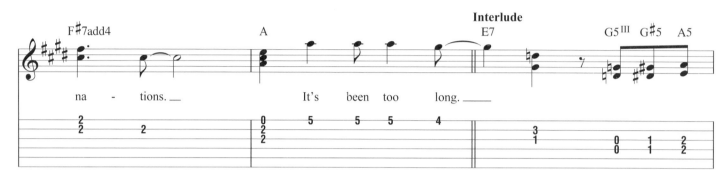

na - tions. ___ It's been too long. ___

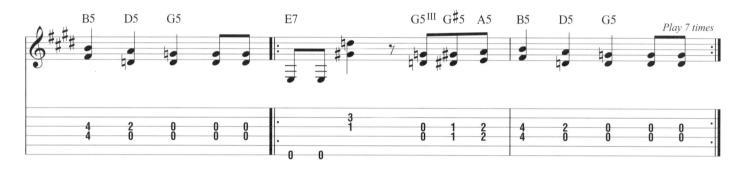

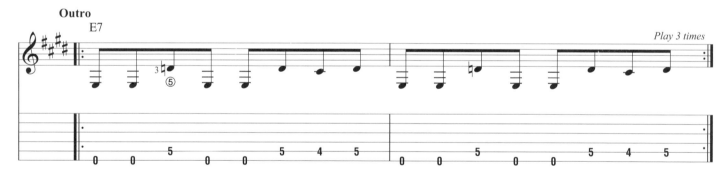

Outro

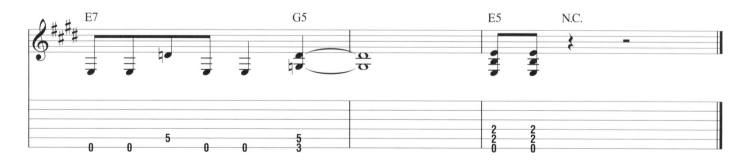

Additional Lyrics

3. Minicyn is pretty, Minicyn is good.
   Seems that all the cysts and mollusks tend to barter.
   Ritalin is easy, Ritalin is good.
   Even all the ones who watered down the daughter.

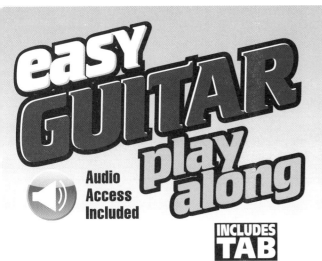

Audio Access Included

INCLUDES TAB

The *Easy Guitar Play Along*® series features streamlined transcriptions of your favorite songs. Just follow the tab, listen to the audio to hear how the guitar should sound, and then play along using the backing tracks. Playback tools are provided for slowing down the tempo without changing pitch and looping challenging parts. The melody and lyrics are included in the book so that you can sing or simply follow along.

1. ROCK CLASSICS
Jailbreak • Living After Midnight • Mississippi Queen • Rocks Off • Runnin' Down a Dream • Smoke on the Water • Strutter • Up Around the Bend.
00702560 Book/CD Pack....... $14.99

2. ACOUSTIC TOP HITS
About a Girl • I'm Yours • The Lazy Song • The Scientist • 21 Guns • Upside Down • What I Got • Wonderwall.
00702569 Book/CD Pack....... $14.99

3. ROCK HITS
All the Small Things • Best of You • Brain Stew (The Godzilla Remix) • Californication • Island in the Sun • Plush • Smells Like Teen Spirit • Use Somebody.
00702570 Book/CD Pack....... $14.99

4. ROCK 'N' ROLL
Blue Suede Shoes • I Get Around • I'm a Believer • Jailhouse Rock • Oh, Pretty Woman • Peggy Sue • Runaway • Wake Up Little Susie.
00702572 Book/CD Pack....... $14.99

6. CHRISTMAS SONGS
Have Yourself a Merry Little Christmas • A Holly Jolly Christmas • The Little Drummer Boy • Run Rudolph Run • Santa Claus Is Comin' to Town • Silver and Gold • Sleigh Ride • Winter Wonderland.
00101879 Book/CD Pack......... $14.99

7. BLUES SONGS FOR BEGINNERS
Come On (Part 1) • Double Trouble • Gangster of Love • I'm Ready • Let Me Love You Baby • Mary Had a Little Lamb • San-Ho-Zay • T-Bone Shuffle.
00103235 Book/ Online Audio.......... $17.99

9. ROCK SONGS FOR BEGINNERS
Are You Gonna Be My Girl • Buddy Holly • Everybody Hurts • In Bloom • Otherside • The Rock Show • Santa Monica • When I Come Around.
00103255 Book/CD Pack.....$14.99

10. GREEN DAY
Basket Case • Boulevard of Broken Dreams • Good Riddance (Time of Your Life) • Holiday • Longview • 21 Guns • Wake Me up When September Ends • When I Come Around.
00122322 Book/ Online Audio........$16.99

11. NIRVANA
All Apologies • Come As You Are • Heart Shaped Box • Lake of Fire • Lithium • The Man Who Sold the World • Rape Me • Smells Like Teen Spirit.
00122325 Book/ Online Audio........ $17.99

13. AC/DC
Back in Black • Dirty Deeds Done Dirt Cheap • For Those About to Rock (We Salute You) • Hells Bells • Highway to Hell • Rock and Roll Ain't Noise Pollution • T.N.T. • You Shook Me All Night Long.
14042895 Book/ Online Audio........ $17.99

14. JIMI HENDRIX – SMASH HITS
All Along the Watchtower • Can You See Me • Crosstown Traffic • Fire • Foxey Lady • Hey Joe • Manic Depression • Purple Haze • Red House • Remember • Stone Free • The Wind Cries Mary.
00130591 Book/ Online Audio........$24.99

HAL•LEONARD®
www.halleonard.com

Prices, contents, and availability subject to change without notice.

EASY GUITAR WITH NOTES & TAB

This series features simplified arrangements with notes, tab, chord charts, and strum and pick patterns.

MIXED FOLIOS

00702287	Acoustic	$19.99
00702002	Acoustic Rock Hits for Easy Guitar	$17.99
00702166	All-Time Best Guitar Collection	$29.99
00702232	Best Acoustic Songs for Easy Guitar	$16.99
00119835	Best Children's Songs	$16.99
00703055	The Big Book of Nursery Rhymes & Children's Songs	$16.99
00698978	Big Christmas Collection	$19.99
00702394	Bluegrass Songs for Easy Guitar	$15.99
00289632	Bohemian Rhapsody	$19.99
00703387	Celtic Classics	$16.99
00224808	Chart Hits of 2016-2017	$14.99
00267383	Chart Hits of 2017-2018	$14.99
00334293	Chart Hits of 2019-2020	$16.99
00403479	Chart Hits of 2021-2022	$16.99
00702149	Children's Christian Songbook	$9.99
00702028	Christmas Classics	$9.99
00101779	Christmas Guitar	$16.99
00702141	Classic Rock	$8.95
00159642	Classical Melodies	$12.99
00253933	Disney/Pixar's Coco	$19.99
00702203	CMT's 100 Greatest Country Songs	$34.99
00702283	The Contemporary Christian Collection	$16.99

00196954	Contemporary Disney	$19.99
00702239	Country Classics for Easy Guitar	$24.99
00702257	Easy Acoustic Guitar Songs	$17.99
00702041	Favorite Hymns for Easy Guitar	$12.99
00222701	Folk Pop Songs	$19.99
00126894	Frozen	$14.99
00333922	Frozen 2	$14.99
00702286	Glee	$16.99
00702160	The Great American Country Songbook	$19.99
00702148	Great American Gospel for Guitar	$14.99
00702050	Great Classical Themes for Easy Guitar	$9.99
00148030	Halloween Guitar Songs	$17.99
00702273	Irish Songs	$14.99
00192503	Jazz Classics for Easy Guitar	$16.99
00702275	Jazz Favorites for Easy Guitar	$17.99
00702274	Jazz Standards for Easy Guitar	$19.99
00702162	Jumbo Easy Guitar Songbook	$24.99
00232285	La La Land	$16.99
00702258	Legends of Rock	$14.99
00702189	MTV's 100 Greatest Pop Songs	$34.99
00702272	1950s Rock	$16.99
00702271	1960s Rock	$16.99
00702270	1970s Rock	$24.99
00702269	1980s Rock	$16.99

00702268	1990s Rock	$24.99
00369043	Rock Songs for Kids	$14.99
00109725	Once	$14.99
00702187	Selections from O Brother Where Art Thou?	$19.99
00702178	100 Songs for Kids	$16.99
00702515	Pirates of the Caribbean	$17.99
00702125	Praise and Worship for Guitar	$14.99
00287930	Songs from *A Star Is Born, The Greatest Showman, La La Land*, and More Movie Musicals	$16.99
00702285	Southern Rock Hits	$12.99
00156420	Star Wars Music	$16.99
00121535	30 Easy Celtic Guitar Solos	$16.99
00244654	Top Hits of 2017	$14.99
00283786	Top Hits of 2018	$14.99
00302269	Top Hits of 2019	$14.99
00355779	Top Hits of 2020	$14.99
00374083	Top Hits of 2021	$16.99
00702294	Top Worship Hits	$17.99
00702255	VH1's 100 Greatest Hard Rock Songs	$39.99
00702175	VH1's 100 Greatest Songs of Rock and Roll	$34.99
00702253	Wicked	$12.99

ARTIST COLLECTIONS

00702267	AC/DC for Easy Guitar	$17.99
00156221	Adele – 25	$16.99
00396889	Adele – 30	$19.99
00702040	Best of the Allman Brothers	$16.99
00702865	J.S. Bach for Easy Guitar	$15.99
00702169	Best of The Beach Boys	$16.99
00702292	The Beatles — 1	$22.99
00125796	Best of Chuck Berry	$16.99
00702201	The Essential Black Sabbath	$15.99
00702250	blink-182 — Greatest Hits	$19.99
02501615	Zac Brown Band — The Foundation	$19.99
02501621	Zac Brown Band — You Get What You Give	$16.99
00702043	Best of Johnny Cash	$19.99
00702090	Eric Clapton's Best	$16.99
00702086	Eric Clapton — from the Album Unplugged	$17.99
00702202	The Essential Eric Clapton	$19.99
00702053	Best of Patsy Cline	$17.99
00222697	Very Best of Coldplay – 2nd Edition	$17.99
00702229	The Very Best of Creedence Clearwater Revival	$16.99
00702145	Best of Jim Croce	$16.99
00702278	Crosby, Stills & Nash	$12.99
14042809	Bob Dylan	$15.99
00702276	Fleetwood Mac — Easy Guitar Collection	$17.99
00139462	The Very Best of Grateful Dead	$17.99
00702136	Best of Merle Haggard	$19.99
00702227	Jimi Hendrix — Smash Hits	$19.99
00702288	Best of Hillsong United	$12.99
00702236	Best of Antonio Carlos Jobim	$15.99

00702245	Elton John — Greatest Hits 1970–2002	$19.99
00129855	Jack Johnson	$17.99
00702204	Robert Johnson	$16.99
00702234	Selections from Toby Keith — 35 Biggest Hits	$12.95
00702003	Kiss	$16.99
00702216	Lynyrd Skynyrd	$17.99
00702182	The Essential Bob Marley	$17.99
00146081	Maroon 5	$14.99
00121925	Bruno Mars – Unorthodox Jukebox	$12.99
00702248	Paul McCartney — All the Best	$14.99
00125484	The Best of MercyMe	$12.99
00702209	Steve Miller Band — Young Hearts (Greatest Hits)	$12.95
00124167	Jason Mraz	$15.99
00702096	Best of Nirvana	$17.99
00702211	The Offspring — Greatest Hits	$17.99
00138026	One Direction	$17.99
00702030	Best of Roy Orbison	$17.99
00702144	Best of Ozzy Osbourne	$14.99
00702279	Tom Petty	$17.99
00102911	Pink Floyd	$17.99
00702139	Elvis Country Favorites	$19.99
00702293	The Very Best of Prince	$22.99
00699415	Best of Queen for Guitar	$16.99
00109279	Best of R.E.M.	$14.99
00702208	Red Hot Chili Peppers — Greatest Hits	$19.99
00198960	The Rolling Stones	$17.99
00174793	The Very Best of Santana	$16.99
00702196	Best of Bob Seger	$16.99
00146046	Ed Sheeran	$19.99

00702252	Frank Sinatra — Nothing But the Best	$12.99
00702010	Best of Rod Stewart	$17.99
00702049	Best of George Strait	$17.99
00702259	Taylor Swift for Easy Guitar	$15.99
00359800	Taylor Swift – Easy Guitar Anthology	$24.99
00702260	Taylor Swift — Fearless	$14.99
00139727	Taylor Swift — 1989	$19.99
00115960	Taylor Swift — Red	$16.99
00253667	Taylor Swift — Reputation	$17.99
00702290	Taylor Swift — Speak Now	$16.99
00232849	Chris Tomlin Collection – 2nd Edition	$14.99
00702226	Chris Tomlin — See the Morning	$12.95
00148643	Train	$14.99
00702427	U2 — 18 Singles	$19.99
00702108	Best of Stevie Ray Vaughan	$17.99
00279005	The Who	$14.99
00702123	Best of Hank Williams	$15.99
00194548	Best of John Williams	$14.99
00702228	Neil Young — Greatest Hits	$17.99
00119133	Neil Young — Harvest	$16.99

Prices, contents and availability subject to change without notice.

HAL•LEONARD®

Visit Hal Leonard online at halleonard.com